From
Mud-Flat Cove
to Gold
to Statehood

From Mud-Flat Cove to Gold to Statehood

California 1840-1850

by

Irving Stone

Word
Dancer
Press

Clovis, California

Quill Driver Books/Word Dancer Press, Inc.
8386 N. Madsen Avenue
Clovis, California 93611
(559) 322-5917

Printed in the United States of America

Quill Driver Books/Word Dancer Press books may be purchased at special prices for
educational, fund-raising, business or promotional use.
Please contact:

Special Markets
Quill Driver Books/Word Dancer Press, Inc.
8386 N. Madsen Avenue
Clovis, California 93611
800-497-4909

To order another copy of this book please call
800-497-4909

ISBN 1-884995-17-9

First Printing May 1999

Quill Driver Books/Word Dancer Press, Inc.
Project Cadre:
Bill Coate
Stephen Blake Mettee
Cindy Wathen
Linda Kay Weber

Library of Congress Cataloging-in-Publication Data

Stone, Irving, 1903-1989
    [Men to match my mountains. Selections]
    From mud-flat cove to gold to statehood : California, 1840-1850 /
by Irving Stone.
        p.   cm.
    Consists of portions of Books 1-3 of: Men to match my mountains.
Garden City, N.Y. : Doubleday, 1956.
    Includes index,
    ISBN 1-884995-17-9
    1. California--History--To 1846.   2. California-
-History--1846-1850.   I. Title.
F864.S7352   1999
979.4--dc21   99-14244
                                                              CIP

For Irving, giving back a little part of what he gave me.

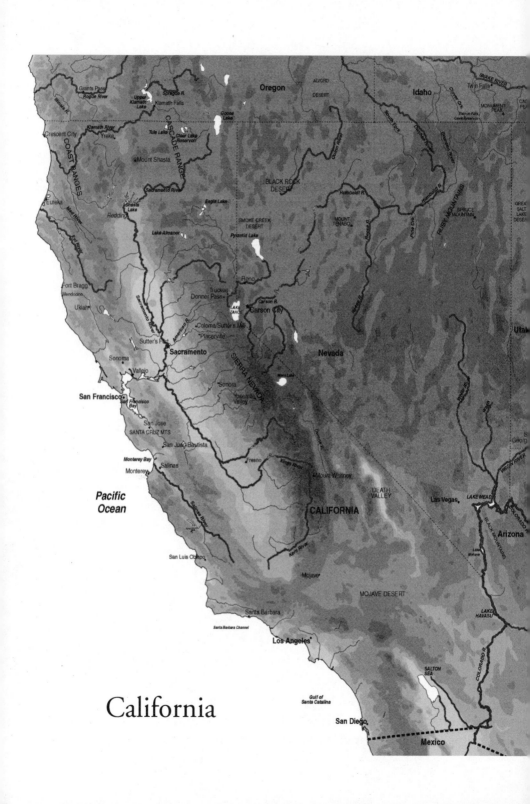

Contents

Foreword

I want to tell a very short, but true, life story.

I first met Irving Stone when I was just out of high school and on my way to the university in Wisconsin. During that summer he said to me, "Don't go to school in Wisconsin, come to school to me. I will give you my B.A. and my M.A. I'm going to write books about all professions; all people—men and women—from all ages and countries, and I promise you that after a few years, you will have very few areas of ignorance left."

I bought it, and I never got such a bargain.

Irving went on to become the master of the biographical novel, and I became his "editor-in-residence." We both believed that the book is the most important tool that man has ever invented—"more important than the wheel, cement or running water." This credo was realized in the more than two dozen books which have enriched, and will continue to enrich, the lives of millions of readers, and which constitute Irving Stone's legacy to the world.

Irving had an abiding love for California. He was born here, he received his formal education here and he lived here. Therefore, it came as no surprise when he said he wanted to write the story of the Far West—California, Nevada, Utah and Colorado. He entitled the book *Men to Match My Mountains*, and it immediately became a best seller.

Now, as California approaches the sesquicentennial of its statehood, a selection from *Men to Match My Mountains* has been comprised to mark that milestone. This sesquicentennial edition includes those chapters dealing with California from 1840 to 1850, that crucial decade in which Mexico's northernmost province was transformed into the thirty-first state of the Union.

Except for its indigenous population—a handful of hunters, trappers and a few hundred settlers on the California coast—the region was totally unsettled and uninhabited. What happened in one region of the West was of tremendous consequence to the other. Their biographies, resources and destinies were so closely bound together, that each was ineradicably woven into the fabric of the whole. For in the beginning, they were one.

This edition is the story of the opening of that land and the building of a civilization. It is a story of the people who contributed. Each life story is an integral part of the mosaic. California, however, is the hero.

Here then is Irving Stone's *From Mud-Flat Cove to Gold to Statehood*. And just as he dedicated all of our books to me, I dedicate this one to him, knowing that through the power of the printed word, he can be with us as we remember California 150 years after statehood.

—Jean Stone

One Man Wants a Wilderness

CAPTAIN JOHN AUGUSTUS SUTTER had cause to be concerned. Had he fled the imminence of a Swiss debtors' prison only to end in a political prison in California? And just at the moment when his colony here in the Sacramento Valley, launched in the teeth of harrowing hardships, was about to be realized?

Though the foreigners who had already been arrested for conspiring to overthrow the Mexican government were hangers-on at the distillery of their leader, the American Isaac Graham, and Sutter had had nothing whatever to do with their loud, sometimes drunken threats to turn California into a republic, still Sutter had only a temporary permit to remain in California. The eleven leagues in the Sacramento Valley, something over seventy-six square miles of land which he had staked out as his empire, would not be legally his until he became a Mexican citizen at the end of his year of residence, in July 1840.

When Sutter had presented himself at the capital in Monterey, just arrived by ship from Honolulu and Sitka, Alaska, with letters of introduction, Juan Bautista Alvarado, California's first native-born governor, had been friendly. Yet from the beginning he had warned Sutter to stay away from the northern frontier because that part of California was "commanded over by Colonel Mariano Vallejo, who could not agree with an adventurous nature coming to the country to live independently."

There was no other way Sutter would have consented to live in California; nor would he have settled for anything less than total wilderness. Captain John Wilson, a Scotsman, who had first sailed into San Francisco Bay in 1833, had thought Sutter out of his mind when he refused to buy at a modest price Wilson's magnificent, stocked ranch in Sonoma Valley, near Mariano Vallejo's settlement thirty miles north.

"Well, my God," Wilson cried angrily, "I should like to know what you really want!"

John Sutter, for the first time in his thirty-six years, knew exactly what he wanted.

"I noticed the hat must come off before the military guard, the flagstaff and the church," he commented, "and I preferred a country where I could keep mine on, where I should be absolute master."

John Sutter's settling of the Sacramento Valley was the result of neither blind accident nor fumbling exploration. Long before his ship came through a narrow unnamed strait into San Francisco Bay and anchored in a mud-flat cove called Yerba Buena, Sutter knew where he was going to found his empire. Before he set foot on California soil he already knew more about the arterial Sacramento Valley than any man living in the Far West. He went to it with the swift, unerring instinct of his colonizing genius.

"I intended to settle in the valley because a captain who had sailed up the Sacramento River for a short distance had told me about the beauty and fertility of that district."

The dozen Americans, Englishmen and Europeans living around Yerba Buena cove had given John Sutter a robustious all-night party on board the *Monsoon*, out of Boston, the only ship in the bay. They were fond of handsome Sutter, the dering-do flare of his semi-military uniform, the flowing hair, and welcomed him heartily to this lonesome frontier where settlers were scarce, cultivated men even scarcer. They wanted him to succeed in his plan. But Dr. John Marsh, whose ranch was on the east side of Mount Diablo, described Sutter's choice as "a settlement in the worst place he could find." Yerba Buena called it "a simpleton's journey" on which there was little chance of success, and in all likelihood would end in disaster and death.

They did not know their man.

John Sutter bought a light ship's boat from Captain Wilson; he also rented the schooners *Isabel* and *Nicolas* from Nathan Spear and William Hinckley, two Americans who owned the Yerba Buena trading post. With credit earned from his sale of merchandise he had brought from Honolulu to Yerba Buena, Sutter loaded his three boats with equipment to start his colony: guns for hunting; ammunition for the cannons he had brought from the islands; seed and farm equipment; blacksmith and carpenter tools.

The little flotilla then set out across the uncharted San Francisco Bay: Sutter, with his title of Captain which he had invented in the same manner that he had conjured up his role of empire builder, the eight Kanaka men and two Kanaka women who had contracted to stay with him for three years and help build his settlement; a fourteen-year-old Indian boy whom he had bought for $100 in the Wind River Rendezvous; a German cabinet-maker; three recruits from Yerba Buena; and several sailors on the beach.

Sutter set out in the lead, four Kanakas rowing the small ship's boat northeast across the wide, choppy bay lying within its frame of soft, sensually shaped hills, haycock tan in the August sun. By dusk they had covered thirty miles, camping where Carquinez Strait emptied into Suisun Bay. The next morning Sutter mistook the San Joaquin River for the Sacramento, and lost two hard days of upstream rowing before he realized that this was not the valley that had been described to him. Several days later he found the mouth of the Sacramento and, leaving messages for his two straggler boats to follow (he placed his messages alongside the Indian tokens of white feathers hanging from bushes to propitiate their gods), made his way up the broad quiet river which flowed between dark jungles of tule and towering trees.

Suddenly he came in sight of a clearing. Several hundred Indians, dressed in full war paint and little else, shrieked their battle cries. But John Sutter understood the Indians; he had lived among the Delawares. Restraining his men who wanted to open fire, he went ashore, unarmed.

"*Adios, amigos*," he said, with his warm, charming smile.

What saved Sutter from a real *adios* at this point was the same quality that was to save him time and again in recurrent tight spots: his lovable, disarming personality. He was a broad-framed, medium height man with a fascinating big-eyed face which managed the miracle of being bland and strong at the same time; a long bony nose, a powerfully rounded chin under which his dark side whiskers met, slashing dark eyebrows, mustaches trimmed neatly and romantically over a fleshy mouth.

The Indian chief, Anashe, liked Sutter's friendly manner; he gave him time to explain that he had come to settle, to be their friend, to show his agricultural implements and samples of the presents he would give to each of the Indians if they would visit him at his settlement.

Sutter had won his first battle of the wilderness by his adroit handling of the natives; but the following day his tired and apprehensive crew threatened to mutiny if he did not turn back. He promptly selected a site just beyond the confluence of the Sacramento and American rivers, put his supplies ashore and announced to the men that all who had no further desire to explore the wilderness could return to Yerba Buena on the two larger boats. He was staying.

Six of the white men decided to return. Sutter gave them a nine-gun farewell salute. William Heath Davis, captain of the returning *Isabel*, reported in *Seventy-Five Years in California*:

"A large number of deer, elk and other animals of the plains were startled, running to and fro, stopping to listen, their heads raised, full of curiosity and wonder, while from the interior of the adjacent woods the howls of wolves and coyotes filled the air, and immense flocks of water fowl flew wildly about the camp."

Left alone with his loyal Kanakas, the Indian boy and Wetler, the German cabinetmaker, Sutter quickly found an elevation about a mile from the river, cut a road to his landing place, began work on a forty-foot adobe brick building divided into a kitchen, bedroom-office and blacksmith shop, then named his little settlement New Helvetia or New Switzerland.

The settlement was a success from the instant of its inception. Sutter organized whole Indian tribes, called "bad Indians" by Governor Alvarado, to hunt and trap for him; wandering French-Canadian trappers joined his settlement; sailors, coming into Yerba Buena after two-year scurvy-laden voyages, heard of Sutter's colony and jumped ship to make their way up the river; Octave Custot, a Frenchman who had worked for Vallejo, joined Sutter as his secretary. His merchant friends gave him credit in supplies and tools with which to make furniture and additional plows.

The land was rich with a plenitude of game for fresh meat. Wild grapes grew in profusion. Although his beaver trappings had not been too successful he had collected some skins to send down to Yerba Buena against his debts. He was passionately in love with the Sacramento Valley, writing to his wife and children in Switzerland, whom he had not seen for almost six years:

"Man can fashion this place into a paradise."

Now paradise was about to be lost.

Now, in the spring of 1840, when he was laying plans to construct a fort which would make his position invulnerable, having sent a group of men some twenty miles up the American River to cut pine trees to serve as giant beams; when he had his Indians making adobe bricks to enclose a rectangular space one hundred fifty by five hundred feet, the walls to be eighteen feet high and three feet thick, with bastions at the corners to house his cannon, with living quarters inside the fort, along the forges, shops, granaries: now Colonel Mariano Vallejo had been ordered by Governor Alvarado to arrest all foreigners and bring them by ship to Monterey, whence they would be sent to Mexico as political prisoners.

He had failed so many times before; all of his life up to this point had been a failure. On July 1, 1839, after five years of continuous wandering he had reached what for him was the Promised Land. It had been a circuitous route: Kandern, Burgdorf, Basle, New York, Cincinnati, St. Louis, Santa Fe, Vancouver, Honolulu, Sitka, and now the Sacramento Valley. His succession of mediocre jobs, the bankruptcy of his shop and humiliating eviction from his home by his wealthy mother-in-law, his business failures in America, all had been wiped out by his bold approach to the unmapped West, his successful organization and sale of the cargo of the *Clementine* in Yerba Buena. There was no longer any doubt in his mind; he knew that he possessed the talent to carve a culture out of the chrysalis of the Far West.

If he were arrested now, and deported, where could he go?

CHAPTER II

A Good Soldier Is Embarrassed

COLONEL MARIANO VALLEJO was as disturbed as John Sutter. He sensed that the arrest of foreigners would reveal the weakness of Mexico's Californio government to the outside world. He knew that the deportation of a group of Americans, Englishmen and Europeans could have serious repercussions; the governments of these men could consider it a breach of international law. California, ignored, neglected, hardly wanted by the Republic of Mexico, had not the strength to resist the feeblest invader.

Vallejo knew Governor Juan Bautista Alvarado very well indeed; they had been raised together in Monterey, and though he was only a year or two older, he was Alvarado's uncle; he had seen how his nephew's ascent to power had made Juan nervous and insecure.

"I was insulted at every turn by the drunken followers of Isaac Graham," complained Governor Alvarado. "When walking in the garden they would come to its wall and call to me in terms of the greatest familiarity. 'Ho! Bautista, come here, I want to speak to you. Bautista here, Bautista there, and Bautista everywhere!'"

No one had ever insulted Mariano Vallejo. Now thirty-one, commander general of the Mexican forces in the north, he had single-handedly founded and built one of the busiest communities in California: Sonoma, in what the Indians called the Valley of the Moon; for, like John Sutter, Vallejo was above all a colonizer. Having been sent north at the age of twenty-three, when he was commandant of the San Francisco Presidio, to learn the reason for the Indian unrest and to investigate the visit of the Russian governor of Sitka to Fort Ross, the Russian settlement on the coast some fifty miles north of the Presidio, the young lieutenant had mounted the crest of a hill and seen spread out before him an undulant valley covered with oaks, manzanita, golden poppies, with superb pasture lands and shining streams. Mariano fell in love at first sight, even as Sutter had with the Sacramento Valley; a year or two later, when he was appointed director of colonization for the north, Vallejo remembered his Valley of the Moon, returning to lay out a square, build barracks for his troops, a two-story *Casa Grande* for himself and his family, break the fields to raise corn and grain: all of this without one *real* of help from either Mexico City or Monterey.

"I could not bring myself to lead the lazy, carefree life so common of the general population," said Vallejo.

He was broadly handsome of face, powerfully built, a grim fighter when aroused, a talented executive with a first-rate intellect, in his own person the bridge between two ages in California. His mother, who came from one of the best Spanish families of California, the Lugos of San Luis Obispo, was described as having a "Puritanic strength of character, imparting to her children a resolute will and an ambitious spirit." Mariano was trained in the tanning of hides, the making of bricks, shoes, cigars; and given a love for books and learning which lasted all his life. At the age of seven he revolted against being forced to learn Ripalda's *Christian Doctrine* at the end of a cat-of-nine-tails, an uprising which he completed at the age of twenty-three when he bought several boxes of books off a ship in Yerba Buena even though he knew they were banned by the clergy who, he said:

"Kept guard over all the ports and bays of California like St. Peter at the gates of heaven, to prevent the entrance of books of a liberal tendency."

Vallejo paid four hundred hides and ten kegs of tallow for his find, worth $1000, thus establishing the best library in California. He had ordered thousands of bricks made of clay and straw, doorways cut from live oaks, stones shaped for archways, red tiles baked to make waterproof roofs, logs hand-hewn to make hardwood floors when even the most prosperous of his countrymen lived contentedly on earthen floors, unleashing a tornado of activity in "pastoral California" where it had been charged that men would do nothing that could not be done on a horse.

Though he had received short shrift from the Mexican government and had been obliged to raise his own army, clothe, feed, arm and pay it, he was passionately devoted to that army, to its rules and appearances as well as its preservation. His father, who had come up from Mexico as a foot soldier in the guard of mission-building Father Junipero Serra in 1774, had been a fractious soldier, constantly in trouble. That was why Mariano had resolved to be a good soldier. Deeply in love with fifteen-year-old Francisca Carrillo, he had waited two full years for marriage because army regulations said that an army officer could not marry without permission from the War Department, and the emissaries he had dispatched over the two-thousand-mile journey to Mexico City were not in as burning a hurry as the young bridegroom. That was why he was stiff-necked and demanding of his ragged and half- starved troops, why outsiders sometimes thought him pompous, pretentious: he stood for the dignity, the integrity, the strength of the Mexican army in California.

Mariano Vallejo had never seen Mexico. His entire devotion was to California, his birthplace, his home, the land he loved. He felt by now that California could never grow nor prosper under Mexican rule, that it was too far away, of no conceivable value or interest to Mexico. He knew also that several foreign governments were keeping a sharp eye on the land: the United States, Great Britain, Russia, France, any one of whom, sending a solitary warship into Monterey, could take the country.

Vallejo liked the foreigners and felt closer to them in mind and temperament than he did to his own countrymen; oh, not Isaac Graham and his cronies, but men like Jacob Leese, born in Ohio, John Cooper, born in England, both men married to his sisters, and owners of ranches in the Sonoma Valley; William Hartnell, the Scotsman who had been his teacher in Monterey.

When John Sutter had come to Sonoma eight or nine months before, bringing messages from his Russian friends in Sitka to their Russian comrades at Fort Ross, Vallejo the soldier had been suspicious of the purpose of a Swiss going to a Russian fort just a few miles from Sonoma; but Vallejo the Californio had liked this dashing, educated foreigner, had extended the bounteous hospitality of a land where there were no inns and every family fed, entertained and bedded strangers who came riding up or down the road, then provided Sutter with fresh mounts and a guide for his journey to Fort Ross.

An astute student of history, Mariano Vallejo sensed that the Far West was rapidly approaching a crisis. He was convinced, after years of total frustration with the Mexican government, that California could only be developed into a great empire if it became American. He was the first and nearly the only native-born Californio to think so.

He was bitterly disillusioned in Governor Alvarado, who had promised to institute all the reforms needed to convert California to a modern province, and had instead taken to drink, become bloated, ill. And now Alvarado had ordered him to engage a vessel in Yerba Buena, arrest all foreigners and transport them to the Monterey jail.

He would obey the order from his commander-in-chief. But it was not a task to his liking.

CHAPTER III

Heroic Frauds, or None at All

NO AMERICAN IN CALIFORNIA had less to fear from these arrests than Dr. John Marsh; and none was more surprised when he landed in Monterey's flea-infested jail. He had come to Los Angeles in 1836 from Santa Fe, taking the westward trail along the Gila River and crossing the Colorado into southern California, had become a naturalized citizen and, when he wanted to buy the cattle ranch at the eastern base of Mount Diablo, had been baptized a Catholic as the law said he must in order to own property in California.

True, he was practicing medicine illegally, having presented his Harvard Bachelor of Arts degree as a medical degree. Since no one in southern California could read Latin, the authorities had granted him a license to practice, thus fulfilling his lifetime ambition. Apparently he had been practicing good medicine, for few of his patients died prematurely. The Californios had little basis for comparison since he was the only doctor in the Far West, and the climate was salubrious. What the Californios knew for sure was that Dr. Marsh practiced expensive medicine: twenty-five cows on the hoof for a professional visit, fifty take-home cows if he had to remain overnight. One outraged housewife deducted twenty-five cows from his bill for washing a couple of his shirts.

John Marsh and John Sutter, now close neighbors in central California, since their settlements were only fifty miles apart, had met in Santa Fe in 1836. Marsh knew that Sutter had as little right to call himself a military captain as Marsh had to call himself a doctor of medicine. Yet on the frontier one perpetrated heroic frauds or none at all. The Far West was little concerned with a man's past: he could become anything he could prove himself to be.

John Marsh, born in Danvers, Massachusetts, weighed two hundred eighteen pounds, stood six feet two in his stockings, was bronzed and powerfully built in spite of his nervous disposition. He was a fierce-looking, ugly man, with the right lid drooping down to cover part of a piercing eye, and two large unabashed warts decorating the crease line from the right side of his nose to the corner of his mouth. The first college graduate to settle in the Far West, he was, characteristically, first to bring a good working library of medical and agricultural books in his saddlebags, these books being his only material possessions. He was thirty-six when he reached Los Angeles, having already lived half a dozen lives. He had hated the grinding poverty of his family's farm, which was barely able to feed the seven Marsh children. Endowed with a vigorous intellect, he was graduated from Phillips Academy at Andover, and worked his way through Harvard by teaching school at Danvers during the winter.

While still an undergraduate John Marsh did extracurricular work in anatomy and worked as an assistant to a Boston doctor. There simply were no funds for medical school, and so he took a tutoring job in the Michigan Territory with a salary which would enable him to save enough money in two years to return to Harvard. He walked off the scene of New England and onto the pages of history: organizer of the first school in Minnesota, Indian agent and friend of the Tribes, compiler of the first dictionary of the Sioux language, a judge in the territory, organizer of Prairie du Chien's defense which averted a massacre.

He fell in love with Marguerite Decouteaux, daughter of a Sioux mother and a French-Canadian father; slender as a reed, with flashing white teeth and a lovely slender face. Marsh took Marguerite into his home as his wife, though no formal ceremony seems to have been performed. Marguerite guided him on his journeys through the wilderness, helped him to write *Rudiments of the Grammar of the Sioux*, bore him a son.

Marsh studied under the army surgeon at Fort St. Anthony for two years, until the medical man died. The tragic break in his life came in 1831 or 1832 when, having been responsible for a retaliatory Sioux massacre of the Fox tribe, he felt obliged to move his wife and six-year-old son southward to the safety of New Salem, Illinois, to protect them from avenging Fox warriors. Marguerite, about to bear a second child, and finding life insupportable without her husband, made her way back, alone and on foot, to Prairie du Chien where she and her infant died in childbirth, both too feeble to survive.

Obsessed with guilt over Marguerite's death, Marsh nearly lost his reason, becoming a wanderer and an outcast. Captured by Indians on the Santa Fe Trail, he saved his skin by extracting an arrowhead from an ailing chief. In Santa Fe he heard of the wonders of California, decided to make his way to Los Angeles and present himself as a practitioner of medicine.

On February 25, 1836, in a one-room mud hut on a sun-baked, sleepy and dusty plaza, thirty-six-year-old John Marsh became Dr. John Marsh. He was busy from the outset, treating smallpox, fevers, hydrophobia, and achieving quite a success as an *accoucheur*. Since he was paid in dried cowhides or tallow, his adobe looked and smelled more like a warehouse than a doctor's office.

Though there was no life for him in the few unpainted adobes around the square, he stayed in Los Angeles for a year, leaving because so few Boston sailing ships stopped in southern California that he could find no market for his hides, piled all the way to the ceiling, and because he thought the country too desert-like for the kind of cattle ranch he envisaged for himself. Making his way north on horseback, he explored the country around Monterey and Yerba Buena, which then consisted of three houses at the foot of a cove so small that it seemed more like the end of a lake than part of the world's largest bay. The biggest of the houses was owned by William A. Richardson, an English sailor who had jumped ship and settled in 1822, now serving as captain of the port for the Californios. Jacob Leese, who later married Vallejo's sister, owned the most popular grocery store in California, for his empty boxes and kegs, set around a stove which kept out the penetrating fogs, became the gathering point for all Americans and foreigners. Marsh moved in with Leese, the two men living on tortillas, frijoles, chile con carne and salt fish. In 1837 Marsh bought the Los Meganos ranch, saying of it:

"I have at last found the Far West, and intend to end my
ramblings here."

The boundaries of the ranch were described in the informal manner of a country with millions of available acres:

". . . from a round-topped hill standing in the range southwest, known as Brushy Peak, to the river, thence following the river to Antioch . . ."

Here John Marsh built himself a three-room adobe hut with an earthen floor, with bulrushes for a roof, furnished with a table, bench and a bed, took an Indian squaw for a housekeeper-wife, made trips of fifty to one hundred miles to attend sick patients. He remained essentially a hermit, taking pleasure mainly from his books, which he read under a huge oak in the yard, building his ranch to fifty thousand acres, five thousand head of cattle, five thousand sheep, still treasuring as his most valuable possession the Harvard Bachelor of Arts degree which he kept locked in a little trunk.

But over the years he was developing a second passion, as great as his love for medicine: a dedication to California and a desire to see it settled by hundreds of Americans who would turn it into a part of the United States. It was a letter he wrote to friends in Missouri which became responsible for the first train to cross the plains to California, precursor of the flash flood of emigrants which would, in one short decade, turn the somnolent and unknown Far West into one of the most talked-about and romantic portions of the earth's globe.

In April of 1840 Marsh went on business to Mission San Jose, some miles to the south. He knew that all the foreigners around San Jose and Monterey were being arrested for the purpose of deportation, but he was a legal citizen, and so he set off undisturbed. Here he was seized by the military and taken as a prisoner to Monterey.

There were some who thought he had been arrested for his fees rather than his fealty.

CHAPTER IV

An Honest Scoundrel Thickens the Plot

UNLIKE "DOCTOR" MARSH and "Captain" Sutter, Isaac Graham presented an honest face to the Far West: he was a scoundrel, he had never been anything but a scoundrel, and he made no effort to dissemble. Leader of the *aguardiente* or saloon set of northern California, he had gathered about him a group of deserters and adventurers who helped him drink up the profits of his still at Natividad, near Monterey. Hubert Howe Bancroft, gargantuan source historian of the Far West, says:

"Graham was the worst of the foreigners, and the cause of all the troubles by his boastful, quarrelsome spirit. He thought he could play hell and turn up jack." An American who had known Graham in New Mexico described him as "noted for being a bummer, a blowhard, a notorious liar." He had come to California over the Old Spanish Trail.

He was a picturesque figure, his face a forest of wild beard and mustache with eyes and nose peering out from the thicket. He wore a wide-brimmed hat at a bravo angle, with a horseman's tie around the collar of his long hunting jacket exquisitely accoutered for the brawl, with a savage hunting knife decorating his belt close to his left hand, a powder horn slung from his shoulder, quickly available to the omnipresent rifle in his right hand.

Yet there was a time when he had almost become respectable: four years before, when Alvarado overthrew the governor sent from Mexico City. Alvarado had enlisted Graham and his rifle-toting friends in his ranks by promising them a bounty of rich lands. Once in power, Governor Alvarado had not kept his promises, and so he had failed to reform Graham, just as he had failed to reform the antiquated government of California.

Isaac Graham's feelings had been hurt. For the past year he had been heard making threats against Alvardo's government. Had not a group of daring Americans taken Texas away from Mexico and set it up as a Republic?

Graham was not saying anything that was not being said more quietly by other Americans in California, but Graham was not always discreet. Tom the Trapper, thinking he was dying, confessed to a priest that Graham was brewing a revolution as well as *aguardiente* in the still behind his hut. In his anxiety Alvarado professed to see a conspiracy. Graham writes quaintly:

"About three o'clock in the morning, I was awakened by the discharge of a pistol, the ball of which passed through my neckcloth. I sprang out of my bed, when they discharged six pistols at me. I had not run four or five yards when they overhauled me with drawn swords, and leveled most deadly and heavy blows at me—which I had the good fortune to evade. Jose Castro then ordered four balls to be shot through me, but was prevented from doing so by an Indian, who continually placed himself as a barrier before me."

Graham was put in chains and carried to Monterey. The only jail in the Far West consisted of a single adobe cell, eighteen by thirty feet, with one small tightly barred window and an earthen floor, damp in the April weather. Alvarado was now embarrassed by finding about forty prisoners crowded into a cell which had previously held only an occasional Indian who had borrowed a horse.

Monterey had been discovered two hundred thirty-eight years before. Cabrillo, exploring the coast in 1542, caught a glimpse of the bay, but did not put in; Sebastian Vizcaino, described as a merchant-explorer, sailed into the bay in 1602, and under one of California's giant oaks gave thanks to God and planted the Spanish flag, naming the spot Monte-Rey, after Spain's viceroy to Mexico. He then made an indigenous error which has come down as inviolable precedent to all California writers: he praised the country in such sonorous superlatives that for the next hundred sixty-seven years all voyagers failed to recognize Monterey from his description.

The name California is the invention of another Spanish fiction writer: one Ardonez de Montalvo, who wrote around 1510:

"At the right hand of the Indies there is an island called California, very near to the Terrestrial Paradise. This island is inhabited by robust dark women of great strength and great warm hearts; when children are born the females are preserved but the males are killed at once, saving only those required to guard against depopulation...."

Portola, in charge of the Spanish soldiers marching north from Mexico in 1769 to protect Father Junipero Serra while he built a chain of missions: San Diego, San Juan Capistrano, San Gabriel, Santa Barbara, Monterey, Carmel, San Jose, San Francisco, Sonoma, passed Monterey twice without recognizing Vizcaino's description. He pushed so far west that he accidentally discovered San Francisco Bay.

Not until the spring of 1770 did Portola find that the adjectives matched the landscape. In 1775 the King of Spain recognized Monterey as the capital of California. By 1803 the first presidio or fort in the Far West had been completed, with barracks, a chapel and homes for the officers. The soldiers as well as the arms were good; no nation made sheep's eyes at the Far West while Spain was acknowledged to be its owner.

As the capital and the only port where foreign ships could declare their cargo, Monterey grew rapidly. As late as 1840, when San Diego was described by visitors as "wretched," Yerba Buena as "squalid," Los Angeles as "the noted abode of the lowest drunkards and gamblers of the country," Monterey had a population of three hundred, some thirty of them Americans and British.

It was the center of the Far West's governmental, social and business world, with the charming whitewashed adobe houses with their red tile roofs built in a semicircle just beyond the white, sandy beach, standing on brilliantly green lawns, the houses covered with flowering vines, pine-covered hills as a background and overhead an Italian-blue sky. There were bullfights on the plaza, dances and fiestas; although there was a law against selling liquor there does not appear to have been any edict against drinking it.

The jail had not been built with an eye to affording a beautiful vista; all the charms of Monterey were momentarily lost on its inmates.

The cell soon became untenable, with the air quite vile, and so crowded that only a few men could stretch out for sleep while the rest stood their turn. Governor Alvarado either had no public money or saw no reason to spend his scarce funds on feeding prisoners who would soon be on the ship chartered by Vallejo to haul them away. As a consequence no food was brought to the prison cell for forty-eight hours.

Since John Marsh had been the most illegally arrested, and was coincidentally the most persuasive talker in the jail, he managed to get himself released by the end of the second day, promising his fellow inmates that he would bring them help. Once out he knew precisely where to go for help: to his old friend Thomas O. Larkin, known as the Yankee from Boston as well as California's first millionaire, the best-liked, or at least the most respected, American in the region.

CHAPTER V

The Time of Action Begins

THOMAS OLIVER LARKIN was thirty years old when he arrived in Monterey. In the eight years that had elapsed he had acquired the first American wife in the Far West, his son was the first American born there, and he pioneered the technique of remaining a Yankee in California while absorbing the privileges of the native Californio. He did a great deal to change the Far West, but the Far West was able to change little in him: the years of living in the warm sun of Monterey surrounded by easygoing, pleasure-loving Californios had imperceptibly slowed his pace, but his New England character had remained impregnable. In the polyandrous marriage of a number of ardent gentlemen to near-virginal California, Thomas O. Larkin was one of the fathers of westward migration.

He was born in Charlestown, Massachusetts, in September 1802, his father's forebears having come over on the *Mayflower* to become freemen of Charlestown in 1638, his grandfather having fought at Bunker Hill in 1775. Losing both parents when he was sixteen, Larkin moved to Boston where he went to work at the noble profession of making books. By the age of twenty he had decided that Boston and New England were too crowded, that he wanted to pioneer. He moved to North Carolina, fitting in so well that within three years he had graduated from stranger and business clerk to merchant, postmaster and justice of the peace.

Larkin had a half brother, Captain John Cooper, former master of the S.S. *Rover* out of Boston, who had settled in Monterey in 1826, married a lovely dark-eyed sister of Vallejo, been baptized into the Church, acquired Mexican citizenship, vast tracts of land and a mill.

Envisaging a similar fate for Thomas, the Larkin collaterals tried to dissuade him from sailing around Cape Horn. They had reckoned without his rocky-coast character: he refused to court the luscious, land-rich but husband-starved Californio girls, refused to take Mexican citizenship or join the Church, though he could have had a land grant of twenty thousand acres almost anywhere in California had he been willing to do so.

Thomas Larkin was not physically robust, nor what one would call a handsome man: his hair was already growing scarce on the frontal dome of his head, he was thin-lipped and thin-nosed, yet his light shrewd eyes were likable. He was a meticulous dresser, wearing his black stock and boiled shirt to business as though he were still in Boston.

Having worked as clerk and bookkeeper in Yerba Buena to get the feel of the new country, he then moved to Monterey and opened his first store on a borrowed $500. He had found the Californios to resemble the North Carolinians; he enjoyed the rare talent for liking strange people and getting along with them. Soon he was not only selling supplies brought in by Boston ships, but had built a flour mill, was contracting to erect buildings with his own lumber and shingles, and had started a vigorous trade in flour, soap, potatoes and sea otter skins.

On the long voyage from Boston to California by the usual route to Hawaii, Thomas Larkin had become friends with twenty-five-year-old Rachel Holmes, born a few miles from him, who was trying to join her husband, a sea captain whom she had married in Massachusetts five years before but had not seen for two years. In Hilo Mrs. Holmes learned that her husband was dead. Larkin, already in love, resolved that Rachel would come to California and marry him. By correspondence he won her acceptance, arranged for her passage to California. He boarded Rachel's ship as it lay outside of Santa Barbara, was married by the American owner of the vessel, who was also United States consul at Honolulu, thus, in a sense, being married on American soil and in a ceremony of their own faith since no ordained Protestant minister had yet set foot on Far Western soil. The new Larkin family remained American, and their progeny would be American too.

Never one to be cavalier with a coin, Thomas Larkin set out to build the first truly American home in the Far West, two-storied, multiwindowed, with wide verandas. He left one set of figures which will wring the heart of every home builder:

	Estimated Cost	Actual Cost
Harry's work	$4.00	$8.00
3500 adobes	20.00	70.00
7 pr. sashes	50.00	70.00
putting up walls	136.00	203.00
2100 shingles	126.00	210.00

The Larkin home became the focal center of newly arrived Americans, Englishmen and Europeans, an unofficial American capital.

From the moment he set foot in Monterey Larkin wanted California for the United States. He pursued California with a combination of efficiency and ardor, as a smart trader who knew that both partners profit from a fair deal. He planned to attach the land, from its Pacific coast to the crest of the Rockies, peaceably, by legal treaty and purchase. Since California was a dead loss to Mexico, and had been ever since Mexican independence in 1821, why should it not negotiate and sell the unwanted territory to the United States for a fair price?

He also knew that few people in the United States yet wanted the country, which had been represented as reachable only by a rough, dangerous seven months journey around Cape Horn or by an equally long, rough and dangerous traversing of thousands of miles of barren, trackless plains, death-dealing deserts and immense mountains.

Larkin had full faith in his own ability and that of men like Marsh and Sutter to persuade people of the beauty and opulence of California despite the hardships of reaching this last outpost, of which he wrote home, ". . . me and my countrymen are living in the farthest West, for we are far beyond what is known by the 'Far West' in the States."

All that was required for this commercial *coup d'etat* was that everyone behave with propriety. But alcohol rather than propriety had been distilled by Isaac Graham, and now Larkin's plan had received a severe setback. Respectable people did not steal millions of acres of land, any more than they stole flour or candles out of a shop.

Helping the prisoners would bring down on him, for the first time in his eight years among them, the disfavor of the native Californios. Yet Thomas Larkin could not abandon his countrymen. He went to Alvarado, secured permission to send food to the men. David Spence, a Scotsman who had come to California from Peru in 1824 to superintend a meat-packing establishment, got permission at the same time to bring in sufficient hides to cover the damp floor. They also secured the release of the non-Grahamites and brought a halt to the arrests. Sutter escaped because Governor Alvarado decided to keep him in the north as a counterforce to Colonel Vallejo.

The one thing that neither Larkin nor Spence could provide was a legal system which would afford the prisoners a trial, witnesses, a jury and a judge. According to Mexican law Governor Alvarado was all of these things rolled into his one badly frightened person.

After thirteen days forty-odd prisoners were taken out of jail and marched between two files of soldiers to the nearby shore, then rowed out to the ship which Vallejo had engaged for the purpose. Graham, in irons, was carried to the boat on the shoulders of several Indians. The entire population of Monterey and inhabitants of the ranches for miles inland were on hand to watch; nothing so exciting had happened since 1818 when the French pirate Bouchard had sacked the town.

No man is such a wretch but that he cannot find a defender. A lawyer from Maine who had gone overland to Oregon, and from there by ship to Monterey, carrying the portentous name of Thomas Jefferson Farnham, arrived the day before the deportation. He wrote in white heat:

"The doors of the prison were opened; its emaciated tenants came out, some of them with no clothing except a ragged pair of pantaloons. The Spaniards had robbed them not only of their cattle, horses, mules, but also of their freedom. Poor old Graham seemed utterly heartbroken."

Farnham cried to Graham as he went by, "Be brave! Let no Tennessean ever think of yielding in this way!"

From his vantage point on the Indians' shoulders, Graham looked down and moaned:

"I can never be a man again. To be chained and exported like a tub of lard, by these here scabs of mankind, is mighty bad."

When Thomas Jefferson Farnham wrote of the deportation in his perfervid style, accusing Governor Alvarado of wanting to get Graham out of the way because he owed him $2235, and published his account in an eastern newspaper, all loyal, red-blooded Americans who read it were outraged. The "bummer, blowhard and liar" who "thought he could play hell and turn up jack" was converted into a national hero.

Soon the small boats plying back and forth had transported the last of their cargo; sail was raised and filled with wind; slowly the *Joven Guipuzcoana* moved out of the bay. Governor Alvarado and the Californios thought that all would now be serene in California.

Captain John Sutter, Dr. John Marsh, Colonel Mariano Vallejo, Thomas O. Larkin, good students all, knew better. This was not an end but a beginning. The white sails dropping gracefully over the horizon were a curtain descending on a prologue known as the pastoral age in California.

CHAPTER VI

John Sutter Takes the Big Plunge

CHIEF FACTOR JAMES DOUGLAS, resourceful head of the Hudson's Bay Company in Canada, raised the curtain on 1841 by appearing on New Year's Day in Monterey Bay with a party of thirty-six trained hunters and trappers which would prove a formidable force in the event the Hudson's Bay company, advance arm of the British government, were in an expansionist mood.

It might well have been; for foolhardy John Sutter had just given the lion's tail a pain-fraught twist. If England were not careful, this stocky blue-eyed Swiss refugee with his camp of Kanakas, Indian allies and a few mechanics might more effectively rid the Far West of the British than the United States Senate had succeeded in doing after years of negotiation over Oregon.

Each spring since 1832 the mountain men of the Hudson's Bay Company had made their way south through Oregon over unmapped trails to trap in the Sacramento Valley; each fall they had illegally portaged back to Canada a small fortune in beaver skins and hides. But the preceding fall John Sutter had informed Douglas that he might never again send his men into the valley, since all of its hunting and trapping rights belonged to him. Nor had Captain Sutter left any doubt but that the next appearance of the Hudson's Bay hunters would bring about a shooting war.

It was a gesture which for nerve had few equals. But it worked. Instead of sending his trappers overland, Douglas brought them down by ship, and applied for official permission to send them into the Sacramento. Governor Alvarado replied diplomatically that Sutter should perhaps have issued a request rather than an order, but now that there was an accredited Californio settlement in the Sacramento Valley, for John Sutter had received his citizenship papers and had been made a minor official of the government, the Hudson's Bay parties must withdraw to more distant fields.

Douglas, who wrote in his journal, "California is a country in many respects unrivaled by any of the globe," was an able maneuverer.

He now requested of Governor Alvarado that the company be allowed to purchase a lot in Yerba Buena, where no one but Mexican citizens could legally own land; to erect a building to house their trading post; to put several of their ships under the Mexican flag, and to naturalize their British captains; thus giving them a "most favored nation" position. Alvarado was amenable.

"I told Governor Alvarado," said Douglas, "that the wishes of the government would be attended to in every particular." To his own people he confided, "We have also other objects of a political nature in view, which may or may not succeed according to circumstances, but in the event of success the results will be important."

He could only have meant: When Mexico loses California we want to be in a position to take the country for Great Britain.

In the wrestling match of history each exertion of force brings forth a counterdisplay: Douglas's securing of special privileges aroused in the Americans in California the fear that they might once again become subjects of England. Not that Great Britain would be so indecorous as to steal the Far West out of the international till, but Mexico owed England $50,000,000 in cash. Why not pay the debt with an unproductive colony? It was to become an omnipresent fear.

Having beaten the British, John Sutter moved on to his second coup. The Russian American Fur Company at Fort Ross, fifty miles up the coast from Yerba Buena, had exhausted after nearly thirty years of too assiduous hunting the sea's supply of otters, those beautiful silver skins which brought up to $200 apiece in Canton. It was ordered to abandon its California experiment and bring the community back home to Sitka, Siberia and Mother Russia. The more valuable personal possessions, rare volumes, costly draperies, art works and piano could be loaded on a ship and taken home; but what about the several cannon, the meticulously built homes, granary, church, the twenty-two-ton launch, four small boats, forty-nine plows, ten carts, harnesses, bridles, seventeen hundred oxen, cows and calves, nine hundred forty horses and mules, two hundred sheep, not to mention the loading facilities of Bodega Bay, close by the fort?

The land itself the Russians could not sell, for they never had had a legal right to settle. They had not recognized Spanish authority north of San Francisco Bay and, knowing that the Mexicans had no army, they had remained, hospitable and friendly neighbors, a bright cultural center with Old World music, beautifully gowned women, brilliant conversation and fine wines. They had even paid the Indians for the lands they occupied; the price was small: three blankets, three pairs of breeches, two axes, three hoes and some beads.

At all times between their arrival in 1812 and their decision to sell in 1840, the Russians were a threat to the possession of California. Provisioning for conquest could have come quickly and amply from Sitka. But the Russians had behaved circumspectly. Now they were preparing to depart, leaving behind formidable resources which could help any nation to become the next owner of California.

Though the Russian American Fur Company had taken out millions in otter skins, it quite humanly wanted to sell its immovable assets at the best possible price. The Russian commander properly offered Mexico the first opportunity to buy. Mexico City assumed that the Russians were moving away in defeat, and ordered Governor Alvarado to occupy the fort, an attitude in which they were encouraged by Alvarado, who informed Mexico City that the Russians would find no purchaser.

The Russian commander next offered the assets to Colonel Mariano Vallejo, his nearest neighbor. Vallejo offered to buy the livestock only. The property was next offered to the Hudson's Bay Company for $30,000. Sir George Simpson, overseas governor of the company, refused to buy on the grounds that they "could not hold the soil, but merely the improvements."

John Sutter now stepped up and offered to pay the full asking price. The Russians liked Sutter: he had been a welcome guest at Sitka. They thought him charming, intelligent, forceful. What if he did not have the $30,000? What if he could barely scrape together $2000 as a down payment? Was he not building a vast empire? Did he not have fields sown with wheat and corn, hunting parties out gathering a wealth of skins; forges, shops turning out goods?

And so they sold to Sutter all the property at Fort Ross and Bodega Bay. The terms were liberal, four yearly installments beginning September 1, 1842, two of $5000 each, the third and fourth of $10,000; the first three payable in wheat, peas, beans, tallow, soap, the fourth in cash.

Had the Russians remained another seven years, until the discovery of gold in 1848, they would have been in position to reach the richest lodes first. Had Mexico bought the cannons and livestock it could have armed and fed its army and put down the Bear Flag Revolt in 1846 at Sonoma, only a day's march from Fort Ross. Had the Hudson's Bay Company bought Fort Ross and Bodega Bay the British could have been so solidly entrenched by the time the Californio government dissolved that California might have fallen quite easily into their hands.

The prize went to John Augustus Sutter, precursor of generations of American plungers, the only man in the Far West with the vision to realize the importance of Fort Ross's assets. Though already deeply in debt to Sir George Simpson of the Hudson's Bay Company, to Thomas O. Larkin of Monterey, to Nathan Spear of Yerba Buena, to his neighboring ranchers, Martinez, Marsh, Suñol, he was possessed of the true gambler's courage which would lead him to treble his debts and put himself in hock for years to come. Yet under the premise of his own planning he was profoundly right; up to this point New Helvetia was a chancy affair. Did he have enough weapons to stave off massed Indian attacks? Did he have the requisite standing to uphold the grants of land he was making freely to newcomers whom he wanted to settle nearby?

Having arranged to move the boats, cannons and cattle to his fort, John

Sutter, son of the foreman of a paper mill and a pastor's daughter, failure as a clerk in a printing house, drapery shop and grocery, who revealed his character by paying twenty-five *livres* for the complete works of Sir Walter Scott while heavily in debt, this same John Sutter had in little more than two years become the most powerful individual in the Far West. Whichever government he threw in with, always providing he did not set up his own empire, would have the inside track for the possession of California.

The move cost him Alvarado's friendship. Jose Castro, military commandant of San Jose, threatened to wipe out New Helvetia. Sutter's naturally red cheeks flamed with anger. He wrote an excited letter to Jacob Leese, the American brother-in-law of Colonel Vallejo.

"It is too late now to drive me out of the country. I will make a declaration of Independence and proclaim California for a Republique."

It was a blustering message, telling of his ten guns and five field pieces, of "50 faithful Indians which shot their musquet very quick." Yet Sutter would have fought and would probably have defeated Castro's ill-equipped soldiers.

Or at least Castro thought so.

Having forced the Hudson's Bay trappers out of California, kept the Mexican government from absorbing without cost the Russian possessions, John Sutter proved himself stronger than the Mexican army and justified his claim to a military title. Captain John Sutter had succeeded in fulfilling what Governor Alvarado described as "the idea of making the Californios believe that he was fate and providence to them."

He was.

CHAPTER VII

"The state of society is exceedingly loose"

RUSSIA HAD SCRATCHED HER entry in the Far West sweepstakes. England, France and the United States were fishing skillfully in troubled waters.

In early May of 1841 France made her entry in the form of an elegant and delightful young attache of the French legation at Mexico City. Eugene Duflot de Mofras, who spoke Spanish, English and German as well as his native French, arrived on the bark *Ninfa* at Monterey with a concealed but challenging assignment: to cover all of California, draw charts of its coastline, rivers and harbors, investigate its soil, climate, resources, make studies of the life and the people; and report everything back to Paris. William Heath Davis describes de Mofras as "a close observer of everything." Just how closely he was observing and for what purpose was revealed only to his government.

"The presidio of Monterey is now entirely demolished, few traces remaining. A small battery stands on the west side of the anchorage. On the sea approach its sole support is a small earthen embankment, four feet high. The battery has neither moat nor counterguard and can readily be approached on all sides...California will belong to the nation that has the courage to send there a corvette and two hundred men...It is the lot of this province to be conquered, and we do not see why France should not collect her part of this magnificent heritage."

The entry of the United States on the scene was late, October 19, 1841, but formidable, taking the form of a flotilla of four armed naval vessels, the U.S.S. *Vincennes, Porpoise, Flying Fish* and *Oregon,* under the command of the Commodore Wilkes. This charting expedition had mapped the hitherto unexplored arctic and antarctic ice fields, as well as the islands of the Pacific. Wilkes had been ordered by his government to put into San Francisco Bay for a sufficient stay to chart the area. Washington had not bothered to secure permission for this survey from Mexico City, nor when Wilkes anchored in the bay did he ask, "By your leave?" a situation somewhat analogous to an auctioneer walking uninvited into a private home while the owner is out, and drawing up an itemized list of valuables which he calculates will one day come under his hammer.

Charles Wilkes was born in New York City in 1798. He had an intensely puritan nature to which all pleasure except that of the intellect was immoral.

Interested in ships from his earliest childhood, he studied navigation and nautical science, shipped out while awaiting an appointment from the navy, at the age of twenty was summoned for his training, sailed the Mediterranean and the Pacific on warships, and in 1838 received command of the exploring expedition.

Wilkes was dedicated to the interests of science and exploring; dedicated men, be they artists or scientists, are rarely social-minded. Unlike the charming de Mofras, Wilkes refused to mix with the Californios, to leave his ship to attend their dinners or balls. He disliked the natives, those of Spanish derivation, with whom he had no contact, apparently watching them from his poop deck with a high-powered telescope.

"The state of society here is exceedingly loose; envy, hatred, and malice, predominate in almost every breast, and the people are wretched under their present rulers; female virtue, I regret to say is also at a low ebb; and the coarse and lascivious dances which meet the plaudits of the lookers-on, show the degraded tone of manners that exists."

His shivering officers "compared the climate to that of Cape Horn with the cold, blustering winds and cloudy skies," but exclaimed over San Francisco Bay:

"This is ours!"

Wilkes was unimpressed.

"The country has by no means an inviting aspect. There are no symptoms of cultivation, nor is the land on either side [of the bay] fit for it. The first view of California was not calculated to make a favorable impression either of its beauty or fertility."

One sentence of Wilkes's report matched that of de Mofras:

"I was surprised when I found a total absence of all government in California, and even its forms and ceremonies thrown aside."

The Wilkes report was discouraging, but one of his orders issued while still in the northwest, designated young fun-loving Lieutenant George F. Emmons to head a party including a navy geologist and artist to make the overland journey southward from the Willamette Valley of Oregon through the mountain country in which the Sacramento River had its course. He also gave permission to a party of twenty-four American civilians, who had come over the Oregon Trail from the east and were awaiting an opportunity to head south for Sutter's Fort, to accompany the navy expedition.

It took the Emmons Party a month to reach Mount Shasta in northern California. They arrived at Sutter's Fort on October 19, 1841. They had suffered hunger and exhaustion, but when it was learned in the East that the entire party, including at least three women and a seven-month-old child, had entered California by the Oregon route in safety, it gave impetus to a pattern of family migration.

The arrival of the Emmons Party also marked the beginning of Sutter's role of *paterfamilias* to all emigrants coming over the mountains. Lieutenant Emmons reported:

"In his brilliant uniform of a Mexican officer and his magnificent presence, he looks as I have in fancy pictured Cortez in his palmiest days. Everything the heart could wish was supplied from the bountiful storehouse of this large-hearted man. Fresh provisions were sent to the camp daily, including fresh-baked bread, milk, fish, groceries and the delicacies our sick and feeble men so much required."

Commodore Wilkes remained in San Francisco Bay only two weeks, then the fleet raised anchor and sailed for Honolulu preparatory to returning home. He remains unique in the story of the Far West for publishing in 1844 the most dismal account of California to be found in the records.

If three nations were staking out Mexico's western lands, in the last analysis it was no one of these government-sponsored expeditions which was to decide the outcome. It was instead a twenty-two-year-old former schoolteacher from Chautaugua County, New York, John Bidwell, who organized and led the first group of emigrants across what had been described as burning deserts, arid plains, impassable mountains and brought them down safely to the ranch of Dr. John Marsh. They had neither map nor guide beyond Marsh's breezy:

"The difficulty of coming here is imaginary. The route I would recommend is from Independence to the frontier rendezvous on Green River, then to Soda Springs on Bear River above the Big Salt Lake, thence to Mary's River until you come in sight of the gap in the great mountain, through that gap by a good road and you arrive in the plain of Joaquin, and down that river on a level plain through thousands of elk and horse. Three or four days journey and you come to my house."

If it sounded easy this can perhaps be ascribed to the fact that Marsh had never come over this route, having entered California by the Old Spanish Trail near the southern border.

The Californios were none too happy over the fact that their coast had suddenly become an international spa.

CHAPTER VIII

"The difficulty of coming here is imaginary"

THE FORMATION OF THE BIDWELL PARTY resulted from the juncture of two streams on the topography of time, neither of which, flowing alone, might have been strong enough to work its way through solid rock.

Dr. John Marsh after his imprisonment in Monterey was confirmed in his earlier opinion that the Californios were incapable of governing their country. To remedy this situation he began writing to friends in Missouri urging them to come to California. One letter was published in the St. Louis *Daily Argus*:

"This is beyond all comparison the finest country and the finest climate. What we want here is more people. If we had fifty families from Missouri, we could do exactly as we please without any fear of being troubled. The difficulty of coming here is imaginary...."

Within a matter of days of the publication of the letter, on October 31, 1840, a French trapper by the name of Antoine Robidoux appeared in the same Missouri county where Marsh's communication was being avidly read and discussed. John Bidwell, big-built, with the powerful patrician head of a Roman senator, listened to Robidoux talk about the Far West.

Bidwell was born August 5, 1819, of English parentage. His biographer describes the Bidwell stock as having "a genius for invention, invincible determination to perseverance, sometimes carried to the point of obstinacy." The boy moved westward with his parents to Erie, Pennsylvania, when he was ten, to western Ohio when he was fourteen. He was principal of a small academy at eighteen, having memorized all of Kirkham's *Latin Grammar* to confound the examining board. Having saved $75 he decided to see something of the western prairies. The $75 and a strong pair of legs carried him through Iowa and Missouri to the Kansas Territory where he taught school for a while, then staked out a claim of a hundred sixty acres. The following summer, 1840, he made a trip down the Missouri River to St. Louis to buy supplies, only to find upon his return that his claim had been jumped. It was at this ripe moment in his life that he encountered the inflammatory words of Marsh and Robidoux. His normally cool nature was set on fire.

"Robidoux's description of California was in the superlative degree favorable, so much so that I resolved to see that wonderful land, and with others helped to get up a meeting at Weston. Robidoux described it as one of perennial spring and boundless fertility.... He said that the Spanish authorities were most friendly, and that the people were the most hospitable on the globe: that you could travel all over California and it would cost you nothing for horses or food. His description of the country made it seem like a Paradise."

Bidwell helped form the Western Emigration Society, pledging along with five hundred other enthusiasts to "purchase a suitable outfit, and to rendezvous on the ninth of the following May, armed and equipped to cross the Rocky Mountains to California." No one knew how to get there, nor yet where California was, except that it was at the extreme west of the Far West, and that one had come to the end when he found himself wading in the Pacific Ocean. The only map Bidwell could find showed two or three rivers as big as the Mississippi River which flowed from Salt Lake into the Pacific. The owner of the map advised young Bidwell to take the tools for building boats!

Then in March of 1841 Thomas Jefferson Farnham, panting defender of Isaac Graham, published a lachrymose letter in a newspaper, his tears washing out the entire Western Emigration Society. . . except John Bidwell.

"Our committee fell to pieces notwithstanding our pledge was as binding as language could make it. When May came I was the only man that was ready to go of all who signed the pledge; and there I was with my wagon!"

As with so many lost causes and lost days, one heroic figure larger than life size can turn a rout into a hard-won victory. In a short time George Hinshaw, an invalid, joined Bidwell on a fine black horse; then Robert H. Thomas and Michael Nye agreed to go; in Weston a wagon with four or five persons joined; at Sapling Grove, the place of the agreed rendezvous, another wagon was waiting for them; then a group of eight men under John Bartleson came in from Independence. Within a matter of five days some sixty-nine men, women and children has assembled, some from as far away as Arkansas. The party was a series of "private messes," held together by the officers they elected: Bartleson as captain, because he refused to join the party unless he was named leader, Bidwell as secretary.

No member of the party had ever been west. No one had a map, an account of the nature of the terrain or the availability of water, food or forage for the animals, for the good reason that none had ever been written. They would have to go it blind.

Then there arrived a group of Catholic missionaries headed for Oregon. They were led by Father Pierre Jean de Smet, who had traveled in the wilderness of the Northwest, guided by "Broken Hand" Fitzpatrick, one of the immortal mountain men of the 1830s. For the next three months, while they crossed the prairie and followed the Platte River through what is now Nebraska and Wyoming, Bidwell and his group learned hour by hour the prairie lore of preservation. At Soda Springs, just north of present-day Utah, the party split, thirty-two of the original Bartleson-Bidwell train deciding to accompany Father de Smet and Fitzpatrick to Oregon. John Bidwell and thirty-one others, including Benjamin Kelsey, his wife and small daughter, resolved to make their way to California. The only advice Fitzpatrick was able to give them was:

"Find the Mary's, follow it to its end, then push west, ever west."

Under the captainship of John Bartleson the party entered on or about August 13, 1841 what is now the state of Utah at a point a few miles north of Ogden's Hole and Great Salt Lake, and began a voyage of inestimable courage. Historians Charles and Mary Beard say:

"Compared to the trials and sufferings endured by this party, the hardships of the voyagers in the *Mayflower* seem positively slight. Certainly the events of this path-breaking expedition, though not as celebrated in annals of history as the doings of the Pilgrims, deserve their vivid chapter in the great American epic."

Bidwell, who had promised a publisher in Missouri he would keep a detailed journal of his travels for the guidance of future parties, wrote as they came in full view of Salt Lake:

"Started early, hoping soon to find fresh water, where we could refresh ourselves and animals, but alas! The sun beamed heavy on our heads as the day advanced, and we could see nothing before us but extensive arid plains, glimmering with heat and salt; at length the plains became so impregnated with salt that vegetation entirely ceased; the ground was in many places white as snow with salt and perfectly smooth—the midday sun made us fancy we could see timber upon the plains. We marched forward with unremitted pace till we discovered it was an illusion."

They killed their oxen for food, abandoned their wagons and equipment, pushed ahead sometimes until midnight, sending out scouts to search for water, grass, game, rivers. On September 7 the party was abandoned by its captain, Bartleson, and his original group, who found the progress too slow, depriving the rest of the company of eight riflemen for protection.

John Bidwell took over, led the party on foot through "valleys between peaks. Having ascended about half a mile, a frightful prospect opened before us: naked mountains whose summits still retained the snows perhaps of a thousand years. The winds roared—but in the deep dank gulfs which yawned on every side, profound solitude seemed to reign."

Reduced to killing their horses for food, then their mules, followed now by hostile Indians, winter began closing in. Bidwell kept alive by eating the "lights" of a wolf, led his people across more mountains, more valleys, more steep, rocky gorges, their shoes in tatters, their clothes in rags, wondering how many more days, more mountain ranges and more deserts away this chimera of California could be.

Only two white parties had made the overland crossing before them: Joseph Walker, in 1833, with a party of thirty-five to forty mountain men; Jedediah Smith, who had entered southern California in 1826 through the Old Spanish Trail, and had crossed the Sierra coming east. The chances of John Bidwell bringing the party through were lessening by the hour.

They had come into Utah by the Bear River, had circled the north end of the Great Salt Lake and struck southwest across the salt desert toward what is today Nevada, seeking the Mary's River. They stumbled into the Mary's in what is now called the Humboldt Valley, made their way down the river to a shallow swamp later called the Humboldt Sink, crossed the Desert Mountains which precede the Sierra Nevada range, then passaged a way up the savage eastern slope of the Sierra Nevada. They were lost for a week in a near delirium of staggering mountain canyons, peaks, unending summits, trying to find their way down the western range.

Bidwell brought his party in, starved, ragged, hollow-eyed but intact. He had been indefatigable, riding through the night to recover lost oxen, struggling down perpendicular cliffs with Indians to purchase their meager supply of acorns, even having the charity to welcome Bartleson back into camp when their former leader cried:

"If I ever get back to Missouri, I would gladly eat out of the trough with my pigs."

On November 1, something over seventy days from their first entrance into Utah and the Far West, Bidwell and his party saw two of their men, Jones and Kelsey, who had gone ahead a week before, come riding up the mountainside. Down in the valley they had come upon an Indian who had spoken one word of English, the one word for which they were thirsting:

"Marsh!"

Three days later, on November 4, 1841, Bidwell led his party onto the ranch of John Marsh, completing successfully the first overland journey of an emigrant party to California.

CHAPTER IX

Schoolteacher Bidwell Lands in Jail

B IOGRAPHY IS NOT ALWAYS A SWEET TUNE, even when played by master musicians.

Dr. John Marsh received the Bidwell Party with great joy: they were old neighbors from Missouri and he was proud, as he wrote his parents in Massachusetts, that "they arrived here directly at my house with no other guide but a letter of mine.... It is an object I much desire, and have long labored for, to have this country inhabited by Americans."

For his welcoming dinner Marsh killed two pigs. He liberally used part of his small supply of seed wheat to provide each of the party with a hot baked tortilla. Grateful for the warmth of their reception, Marsh's guests proffered him gifts from their equally scanty possessions: a few cartridges, a butcher knife, an inexpensive set of surgical instruments. Marsh gave his bedroom to the Kelsey family, spread cowhides over the earthen floor to bed down as many as the adobe would hold. Before bidding his friends good night, he invited them to kill a beef to roast over their breakfast fire.

The next morning Marsh went out into the yard to find that Bidwell and his friends had mistakenly slaughtered and largely devoured his best-trained work ox. The affable host of the previous evening was replaced by an angry and acidulous stranger who cried:

"The company has already been over a hundred dollars expense to me, and God knows whether I will ever get a *real* of it or not."

Bidwell took his people into conference. They decided to leave Marsh's at once, half of them to hunt and trap in the San Joaquin Valley, the rest to seek out the town of San Jose to find work.

When fifteen of the party reached Mission San Jose they were arrested by subprefect Antonio Suñol and put in jail for entering Mexican territory without a passport. Colonel Mariano Vallejo was staying at the mission. As an admirer of Americans he was delighted to learn that they had forced the Sierra Nevada and intended to settle in California. As the commanding general of the northern territory he had to take official alarm at this band of armed men, constituting a military forces as large as his effective army. Informed that they had made the trek at Marsh's importuning, Vallejo dispatched one of the party to bring Marsh on the double.

Marsh went bond for fifteen members, Vallejo himself graciously went bond for another five, whom he invited to go to his hacienda in Sonoma, there to be housed as his guests until they could find work or buy land. Apparently Marsh did not ask for a passport for John Bidwell. When Bidwell found that there was no passport for him, he quarreled with Marsh, then made his way to the Mission San Jose. Here Suñol arrested him.

"I was marched into the calaboose and kept there three days with nothing to eat. There were four or five Indians in the prison, they were ironed, and they kept tolling a bell, as punishment, for they were said to have stolen horses."

While in jail Bidwell learned that the Emmons Party which had reached Sutter's Fort just sixteen days before had suffered no such flea-bitten reception on the part of the authorities. They had put themselves under the protection of Captain John Sutter who, as a Mexican official with loosely defined powers, regally assumed that he had the right not only to issue passports to all new arrivals, but to make them grants of land in the Sacramento Valley as well.

Bidwell finally attracted the attention of Thomas Bowen, an American living in San Jose, who went bond for him and secured his passport from Vallejo. His three days in the calaboose had embittered him. When he left for Sutter's Fort, where he was told he could find work, he carried with him a lifetime hatred for John Marsh; the first of a legion of quarrels between settlers which was to turn the tranquil, gracious Far West into a land of brawling violence.

The men of the Bidwell Party, the first caravan to make the direct overland crossing to California, settled in the Sacramento and San Joaquin valleys and the rich lands between Yerba Buena and San Jose, to dig their heels resolutely into the native earth and play, each in character, his part in the uprising, the war, the formation of a new state and a new culture.

As 1841 drew to a close a third emigrant train reached California. John Rowland, William Workman, Benjamin Wilson and a group of Americans living in Taos and Santa Fe under Mexican rule had been making a living as traders and trappers for some ten years, Wilson having moved down the Santa Fe Trail for purposes of his health. Some of them had been in correspondence with the leaders of the Texas uprising; there was talk of a Texas expedition coming in to take New Mexico and join it to Texas. In the summer of 1841 the government of New Mexico got wind of the conspiracy and, says Wilson:

"Under the circumstances Rowland and Workman and myself, together with about twenty other Americans, concluded it was not safe for us to remain longer."

The Workman-Rowland Party made up at Abiquiu, high in the north central part of New Mexico, a few miles from Taos. In it were two men, Isaac Given and Albert Toomes, who had arrived at Sapling Grove, Missouri, too late to join the Bidwell Party, a number of New Mexico traders as well as a group of scientists whose purpose was to study the terrain, and several Mexican women. A flock of sheep were driven along the trail to supply food.

The party left in the first week of September to avoid the worst of the desert heat, their route being sharply northwest. Within a few days they were cutting across the southwest corner of present-day Colorado. Continuing northwest, they crossed the Colorado River, then the Green and the Sevier, separated by only twenty days and two hundred miles from the suffering Bidwell train.

The Old Spanish Trail turned sharply south, following the Sevier and then the Virgin rivers through the overpowering, brilliantly hued cathedral spires of what are now Bryce and Zion National Parks, across the Mojave Desert, over Cajon Pass and down into the milk and honey and orange groves of the San Gabriel Mission, the trail constituting roughly what is now the main highway from Salt Lake City to Los Angeles.

In contrast to the harrowed diary of John Bidwell, Benjamin Wilson, who was going to California only because he wanted to catch a ship for China, confined his total description of their voyage to one sentence:

"We met with no accidents on the journey; drove sheep with us, which served us as food, and arrived in Los Angeles early in November."

Rowland took a list of his company into Los Angeles, where the authorities issued permits for the party to stay. Workman and Rowland, because they had Mexican wives and had become Mexican citizens in Taos, were permitted to buy the Puente ranch in the San Bernardino Valley; Benjamin Wilson, refusing to give up his American citizenship, still felt free to buy the Jerupa ranch, even though he was on his way to China.

In 1841 three separate emigrant trains had made their way to California. But Sir George Simpson, head of the Hudson's Bay Company, managed to get in the closing word for Great Britain. On December 20 Simpson, arriving on a round-the-world tour, observed:

"English, in some sense or other of the word, the richest portions of California must become. Either Great Britain will introduce her well regulated freedom of all classes and colors, or the people of the United States will inundate the country with their own peculiar mixture of helpless bondage and lawless insubordination."

Sir George may not have been the most tactful visitor in California, but one must admire him for his forthrightness.

CHAPTER X

A Fort Plays Host

W HEN JOHN SUTTER LEARNED that the Bidwell Party was floundering its way down the Sierra Nevada he had loaded two mules with provisions and sent two of his men to guide the emigrants to safety at the fort. No contact had been established. Now it took a week of hard slogging for John Bidwell to make the hundred-mile journey to Sutter's, for it was the height of the rainy season.

"Streams were out of their banks, plains were inundated. Game was plentiful but hard to shoot in the rain; it was impossible to keep our old flintlock guns dry, and especially the powder dry in the pans."

The hardships of the journey were forgotten in the warmth of Sutter's welcome, with hot food, strong brandy, companionship and offer of employment. John Bidwell, who went to work for Sutter, reported, "As long as he had anything he trusted everybody with it, friends and strangers alike. Always liberal and affable, his establishment was a home to all Americans, where they could live as long as it suited them without charge. Everybody was welcome—one man or a hundred."

One of Sutter's biographers comments:

"He was one of those Falstaffian creatures that live for the sensation and tickle of being alive. His entire physique was a radiating mass in which the joy of life became contagious. Therein rested the fascination of his personality which, in its best moments was a marvel of nature, a lusty phenomenon like an enchanting cataract, a geyser or a magnificent thunderstorm."

It was an important part of Sutter's concept that he must get his fort completed and impregnable before somebody decided he had grown too strong and had better be driven out. He had sent supplies to the Bidwell Party not only to afford succor but to bring the party into New Helvetia where the men could enter his employ as trappers, mechanics, farmers, soldiers. He had no money to pay them, but he could offer them the more important compensations of food, shelter, protection and ultimately a grant of land, not altogether legally, but who in the Californio government would be strong enough to take it away?

When Bidwell reached Sutter's on January 28, 1842, he found the fort pretty well finished, with bastions above the walls to command the gateways, its Honolulu and Fort Ross cannons sitting before the entrance. Inside the fort, utilizing the back of the main wall, were a number of rooms used for sleeping, cooking and eating, a blacksmith shop, tannery, storehouse and still. At the enter of the fort were corrals and dwelling houses. Sutter now had in his employ about thirty foreigners, among them Robert Ridley, a cockney who ran the boat on the river. Ridley, known as "the most facile, artistic, bare-faced liar in California," was liked by Sutter because he played a good game of whist. Perry McCoon was the overseer of the stock; William Daylor, a former sailor, was the cook; Frenchman Custot still acted as Sutter's secretary. There were two Germans, Nicolaus Allgeier and Sebastian Keyser, Pablo Gutierez, who had been with Sutter on the Santa Fe Trail, and Joel Walker, who had come from Oregon with the Emmons Party. Sutter still had his eight loyal Kanakas and the two Kanaka women. Former mission Indians made adobes; several hundred untamed braves were herded in by their chiefs to till the ground with crude pointed sticks. The Indians were fed in the open court, out of wooden V-shaped troughs which were filled with a hot gravy-mush made of bran with scraps of meat and vegetables. The Indians kneeling on either side of the troughs scooped the oozing mixture into their mouths with their hands.

Sutter sent John Bidwell to Bodega Bay to help ship the supplies from Fort Ross. Joseph Chiles of the Bidwell Party returned to Missouri to get his family, carrying Bidwell's chronicle of the journey west. Once published it spread widely the news of the women and children who had gone through safely to California.

But Chiles departed a little too soon to carry another interesting bit of news: in March of 1842 a Mexican laborer, pulling wild onions on the land of Ignacio del Valle in the northern section of the San Fernando Valley, found a pebble that contained a metal which looked like copper but proved to be gold. A number of Mexicans from Sonora explored the land. They found that by washing out the gravel of the Santa Clara River as well as the sand and earth of the land drained by the river they could placer about $2.00 worth of gold a day. Thinking there might be a rush, the prefect of Los Angeles appointed owner del Valle as justice, with the right to charge a rental fee on the land being washed.

The $2.00 a day dwindled to a few cents; few Mexicans continued with the unrewarding chore.

CHAPTER XI

"*There is no man to whom I owe as much as Fremont*"

ON JULY, 9,1842, there arrived in northeastern Colorado the most controversial character ever to fight his way into the Far West: a small, lean, handsome, wiry, indefatigable, melancholy-eyed, near genius who, a full century after his part had been played, was still raising dust storms of printed partisanship among biographers.

Lieutenant John Charles Fremont, of the United States Topographical Corps, twenty-nine years old, married to the most brilliant girl in Washington City, Jessie Benton, daughter of the western-expansionist senator from Missouri, Thomas Hart Benton, was now leading a third government expedition into the West. Unlike Captain Zebulon Pike and Major Long, who carried trained soldiers with them, Lieutenant Fremont was the only army man in his expedition. The balance of his party, assembled in St. Louis and on the Mississippi River, consisted of civilians paid by the army: a topographer, a hunter, nineteen French voyageurs, all experienced fur trappers; and most important, a medium-height, broad-shouldered, clear-eyed mountain man, the contemporary and equal of Jim Bridger and Broken Hand Fitzpatrick: Kit Carson, who served as guide. Between Fremont and Carson there sprang up a deep and abiding friendship.

Fremont said, "Carson and Truth are one."

Carson said, "There is no man to whom I owe as much as Fremont."

Together, during three expeditions filled with discovery, danger and violent death, they did more to explore, map and publicize the routes to the Far West than any combination in the expansionist years.

John Charles Fremont was the illegitimate son of a Royalist French émigré teacher and a high-born Richmond, Virginia, woman married to an aged Revolutionary War hero named Pryor. Fremont was born in Savannah, Georgia, and grew up in poverty. A brilliant student in scientific subjects, he became an assistant with the U.S. Topographical Corps on a railroad mapping expedition, and another to the Indian frontiers of the Cherokees. Through a friendship with Secretary of War Poinsett he became a second lieutenant in the Corps in Washington City where he was trained by Joseph Nicollet, the country's ablest cartographer, who took him as an assistant on an expedition into the Indian country of the upper Missouri.

By the time he was twenty-seven, he and sixteen-year-old Jessie Benton were deeply in love. Separated by an order, arranged for by Senator Benton, to explore and map the Des Moines River in Iowa Territory, Fremont returned six months later to marry Jessie without her parents' consent. Senator Benton stormed, then welcomed his son-in-law into the Benton home, westward-expansion center of Washington City. Most of the Congress was indifferent to acquiring such distant territories as Texas, Oregon and California. Senator Benton pushed through a bill to map the route to Oregon, and John Fremont was named to head the expedition.

What the Congress and President Tyler did not know was that neither Benton nor his dynamic young son-in-law had the slightest intention of stopping at a map for Oregon. They would not be content until they had discovered and established new routes along which thousands of American families could travel to settle the Far West and claim it for the United States.

Fremont spent less than a week in Colorado on his first expedition. He wanted to explore the Rockies for a shorter, quicker pass into California, but his orders obliged him to turn sharply north in order to map South Pass, above the present Colorado-Utah state lines. He determined to return the following year. Upon that iron-willed determination much would hinge, including the heroic Mormon trek to Great Salt Lake: for when Brigham Young, ill with mountain fever, rose up on one elbow in the lead wagon, in the hills above the Salt Desert, and said to the driver:

"This is the place!" he meant, in part:

"This is the place described by Lieutenant Fremont."

Chapter XII

Commodore Jones Goes out on a Yardarm

A MONTH AFTER John Fremont left the northern border of Colorado there appeared in San Diego Harbor the last of the Mexico City governors for a remote and increasingly troublesome colony: handsome General Micheltorena, who had fought under General Santa Anna, now President of Mexico, against the Texans. Micheltorena arrived with an army of some three hundred fifty men on three ships, largely in reply to the realistic reports of Colonel Mariano Vallejo to the effect that he had had no military force large enough to repel the Emmons or Bidwell parties, or the larger expeditions reported on their way. California, insisted Colonel Vallejo, could no longer be held for Mexico without trained, armed and well-financed troops. But when the *Chato* unloaded its soldiers and their families, one of the Americans watching the operation gasped:

"They presented a state of wretchedness and misery unequaled. Not one individual among them possessed a jacket or pantaloon, but naked and like the savage Indians, they concealed their nudity with dirty miserable blankets. The greater portion of them had been charged with the crime of either murder or theft."

Aside from having no arms with which to soldier, a trade for which they had no stomach, the troops had no commissary and Micheltorena no funds with which to feed them. Soon the hungry legion had spread over southern California like a plague of locusts, stripping the countryside bare of food, a task for which the anguished Angelenos claimed they had plenty of stomach, indeed.

The Mexicans were not the only ones making a show of military strength in the fall of 1842; the Pacific Ocean was awash with warships: the United States was represented by five ships with one hundred sixteen guns; the English by four ships with one hundred four guns; the French by eight ships with two hundred two guns. Commodore Thomas Ap Catesby Jones of the U.S.S. *United States*, in charge of the American flotilla, had orders from the Secretary of the Navy:

"The unsettled state of the nations bordering on the coast included in your command, renders it necessary to protect the interests of the United States in that quarter." However, "Nothing but the necessity of prompt and effectual protection to the honor and interests of the United States will justify you in committing any act of hostility."

Commodore Jones was out on a yardarm: if he let the prize of California fall into British or French hands he could be court-martialed for the treason of inaction; if he moved boldly in to seize California he would even more quickly be fed to the sharks.

In the beginning of September, returning with his flotilla from a cruise, Commodore Jones was faced with three decisive pieces of evidence: the British fleet was sailing under sealed orders; a letter from the United States consul at Mazatlan informed Commodore Jones that a war with Mexico over the annexation of Texas was about to break; a Boston paper carried the story that Mexico had ceded California to England to cover a $7,000,000 debt. Commodore Jones conferred with the United States consul at Lima, then with the commanders of his three ships. All agreed:

"Strike! Strike swiftly!"

On October 19, 1842 Commodore Jones reached Monterey. He was intensely relieved to find that the British had not preceded him. Believing that Micheltorena's army marching by the overland route was within close range, the commodore sent one of his captains ashore to demand the surrender of the government.

The Californios had no armed troops in their capital. The two most astonished and hurt people on shore were Governor Alvarado and Thomas O. Larkin: Alvarado because he was being stripped of office; Larkin because he believed his countrymen were behaving in a highhanded fashion.

At midnight Larkin accompanied two Californio commissioners to Commodore Jones's ship. The articles of capitulation were drawn up, Larkin serving as interpreter. At nine the next morning they were signed; at eleven, Commodore Jones sent one hundred fifty sailors and marines ashore. The Mexican flag was lowered at the fort. The American flag was raised, the first to fly in the Far West.

Commodore Jones was happy that the conquest had been bloodless. His happiness was short-lived. Thomas Larkin showed the commodore recent newspapers and commercial letters from Mexico, proving that Mexico and the United States were waging a cold war rather than a hot war.

"This change in the aspect of international affairs called for prompt action on my part," cried Commodore Jones. To the Californios he said, in effect:

"Ooops, sorry!"

He issued orders to haul down the American flag. The Mexican flag was raised in its place. To show there were no hard feelings, Jones had his guns fire a salute of honor.

Thus, in October of 1842, the United States was in possession of California for about thirty hours. Larkin, who believed with all the passion of his neat and orderly business soul that California could be purchased peaceably from Mexico, returned to his sumptuous home, relieved. Commodore Jones wrote:

"I may forfeit my commission and all that I have acquired in seven and thirty years' devotion to my country's service."

According to eyewitness accounts, the Californios appeared more surprised and pained by the return than by the capture; Alvarado's treasury was empty, all salaries seriously in arrears. When the natives of southern California heard of the conquest they asked only two questions:

"Will they meddle with our ranches? Will they interfere with our religion?"

The high-spirited Californio women were far more resentful than their men, the female of the species frequently being more touchy and violent than the male when it comes to causes and loyalties.

As the military commandant of the northern section, Colonel Vallejo should have been outraged at Commodore Jones. Officially he was. But when the commodore made a trip to Sonoma with a group of his officers, Vallejo found that he liked the American naval commander enormously, entertaining him with a full day of rodeo and Indian dances, and forever after spoke highly of the first American officer to claim California for the United States.

It was Governor Micheltorena in Los Angeles who had the final word: after keeping Commodore Jones dangling for three months in anterooms in Monterey and Yerba Buena, the governor decided to open the New Year of 1843 by permitting the commodore to submit his official apology. On January 19 the Mexican government gave the American officers a formal ball of forgiveness.

Governor Micheltorena asked as reparations for the grievous insult $10,000 in cash, eighty new military uniforms, and a set of instruments from the band on board the U.S.S. *United States*, thus ending the untimely incident on a note of musical comedy.

CHAPTER XIII

£1,000,000 to Drive out the Americans

ABOUT JUNE 20, 1843, a twenty-four-year-old lawyer by the name of Lansford W. Hastings, from Mount Vernon, Ohio, a bright, handsome, strongjawed, fast-talking opportunist, reached the northern California border, where the Shasta River crosses into Oregon. The previous spring Hastings had turned up at Elm Grove, Kansas, twenty miles west of Independence and joined the Reverend Elijah White's party of approximately one hundred sixty people starting for Oregon. Within a few days brash, aggressive Hastings, a tenderfoot with little or no frontier experience, had managed to replace the veteran Dr. White as head of the expedition! However, a few miles out of Fort Laramie, Dr. White hired Broken Hand Fitzpatrick to lead them to the Willamette Valley in Oregon.

The following spring Hastings was moving energetically about Oregon, successfully selling a California he had never seen to a group of fifty-three settlers, twenty-nine of them armed men, the rest women and children.

"Myself again having been honored with command," he wrote, the party set out on June 1 with a guide for Sutter's Fort. Somewhere on the Rogue River, two or three days distance from the border, they were met by a party from California driving a herd of cattle north to sell. Their stories of life in California were so discouraging that Hastings lost his guide and almost half his party. Not at all abashed, he followed the route used by Emmons in 1841 through the present Grant's pass, down a tributary of the Rogue River, skirted Shasta Lake, followed the Sacramento River flowing south out of the lake until he reached Sutter's.

The journey had taken forty traveling days. Where Emmons had managed to avoid fights with the Indians, Hastings had several battles, one on the Shasta, another in the Sacramento Valley, one of his men emerging with an arrow in his back. Nonetheless he made a safe crossing. With nine hundred people migrating from the Missouri border to Oregon in the year of 1843, the Hastings passage not only meant that many more emigrants to Oregon would essay the southern journey to a warmer, drier California; it also established Lansford W. Hastings as a leader and guide . . . at a future cost of human suffering unequaled in the annals of man's anguish.

When the party reached the bank of the Sacramento River opposite Sutter's on July 10, a young couple impetuously crossed the river to have Sutter marry them instanter; the balance of the party made the crossing the next day, to be heartily received by Sutter who:

"Rendered every one of the party every assistance in his power."

Captain John Sutter was by now an outsized figure on the landscape. His fort was complete, a marvel in the wilderness, he was governing a self-sustaining community with blacksmiths, gun-smiths, carpenters, shoemakers, a gristmill, weaving shops. He was known in the East not only as host and helper of Americans coming into California, the growth in his power indicated by the belief that he had the right to marry people, but as overlord of an empire.

Yet Sutter, with all his military prowess, imagined and real, had been able to conquer neither the mosquitoes, the fleas, nor that most formidable of all bloodsucking insects, debt: like most visionaries he had overextended himself. The money he owed to Larkin in Monterey or Nathan Spear in Yerba Buena, or Vallejo, he was not being pressed for: these men liked him, believed in the importance of his empire in the wilderness. But Sutter had suffered an intense year of drought and had no grain to pay the Russians; his tannery was not yet working successfully, the brandy of his distillery was still raw. He had accomplished a miracle of building in three years, creating the beginnings of modern-day Sacramento in the midst of an unexplored virgin forest; but the larger he grew, the more he fell in arrears.

Perhaps Sutter used these debts as an excuse for not sending for his wife and children in Switzerland; an untoward accident had forced the Sutters into a marriage neither of them had wanted or enjoyed. A journal written in German by Heinrich Lienhard, Sutter's major-domo during this time, insinuates that both of the Kanaka women whom Sutter had brought from Honolulu had served as substitute wives, while one of them, Manaiki, was said to have borne him several children. Lienhard also suggests that Sutter had several children by a number of the squaws at the fort. In contrast to John Chamberlain, the Irish blacksmith of the fort, however, Sutter seems abstemious: Chamberlain apparently married nineteen Indian women in swift succession.

If John Sutter did not meet his payments, the Russians could move into the Sacramento Valley and take over the fort, establishing a new base in the Far West; this time they would have rich agricultural lands behind them and the strategic position to repel all American migration coming south from Oregon or west from Missouri.

Sutter also had William Rae, representative of the Hudson's Bay Company, on his mind. Rae was being a bit stuffy about the money Sutter owed his company and had started legal action against him in an effort to attach either his boats or produce, a step which the residents considered most unfriendly and considerably less than cricket. Rae had been heard to say, while in his cups, that it had "cost the Hudson's Bay Company £75,000 to drive the Yankee traders from the Columbia" and that they would "drive them from California if it cost a million."

The international situation now seemed to depend on how much wheat John Sutter would reap and harvest before his next payment to the Russians came due; and how successfully he could keep the Hudson's Bay Company from possessing his fort.

CHAPTER XIV

Wagons? Impossible!

ON MARCH 1, 1843, John Charles Fremont submitted the report of his expedition along the South Platte River in Colorado to Colonel Abert of the Topographical Corps, and to the Congress. The House not only ordered the report published but authorized a second expedition, this time to go all the way to Oregon on its combined map-making, exploring voyage.

Fremont now stepped forth with considerably increased confidence and power: this time Congress had authorized him "to connect the reconnaissance of 1842 with the surveys of Commander Wilkes on the coast, so as to give a connected survey of the interior of our continent." Commander Wilkes had mapped San Francisco Bay and the Sacramento River as far as Sutter's Fort.

Fremont, without the knowledge or consent of the Topographical Corps, took along a twelve-pound howitzer. Senator Benton believed war with Mexico would in all likelihood begin by the time Fremont reached California; and Fremont had every intention of leading his group of thirty-nine armed, hard-bitten frontiersmen into action.

But at the moment there was exploratory work to be done: to find and chart a route through the Rockies of central Colorado which would save the emigrant trains many hard days of travel. On July 4 he and his men set out almost due south, along the comparatively easy route which now connects Greeley, Denver, Colorado Springs and Pueblo, remaining in American territory, but carefully studying the mountains to the west which led to the Mexican holdings that extended one thousand miles to the Pacific.

Colorado was beginning to make its transition from an outpost country to that of settled communities: Fort Lupton, ten miles down the river from St. Vrain's trading post, was a well-stocked farm, growing vegetables, raising cattle, hogs, turkeys and chickens; at the other end of Fremont's trek south, where Boiling Spring River enters the Arkansas, Fremont found a fair-sized community of former hunters and trappers who were farming and ranching, having successfully albeit reluctantly made the transition from mountain men of the thirties to settlers of the forties.

Here Fremont was joined by Kit Carson. He had also hired Broken Hand Fitzpatrick. Neither Carson nor Fitzpatrick had heard of a pass through the Rockies. Fremont sent Fitzpatrick with the wagons and howitzer along the northern route to Fort Hall, while he, Carson and twelve men turned west. For five days they struggled through "scenery very wild and beautiful. Towering mountains rose round about, their sides sometimes dark with forests of pine, and sometimes with lofty precipices. The green river bottom was covered with a wilderness of flowers."

On August 1 they crossed into what is present-day Wyoming. A month after Fremont withdrew his expedition northward, the most important emigrant party of 1843 came southward from Fort Hall, in present Idaho, into the extreme northeast corner of Nevada, headed for the Mary's River. The party was led by one of the greatest mountain men of his era, Joseph Walker, who ten years earlier had explored the region west of Salt Lake forcing a passage through the mountains to the coast. Walker was now assaying the task of leading a caravan of heavy, slow-moving wagons across the salt desert trail and wall of mountains that had been traversed by the Bidwell Party on foot.

The daring idea was conceived by Joseph B. Chiles, who had crossed with Bidwell in 1841, returned over the Sierra Nevada in 1842. He bought an entire mill, boxed the separate parts to be loaded into a wagon, and then assembled a party of about fifty to accompany him on his return to California. Chiles's wife had died, a misfortune which had sent him wandering to find a new land and a new life just as ill-health, business failure, lack of opportunity, boredom or sheer hunger for travel and adventure, as well as free lands, would send so many thousands.

When the Chiles Party reached Fort Hall it was late in the season, August 27. Chiles, resolving to lighten the expedition, decided to take nine men with him on horseback, go northwest to Fort Boise, then cut southwest through a route suggested by the hunters, coming into California at its northeast corner. He entrusted his wagon, with everything he owned in the world invested in the disassembled mill, to Walker's care, to be brought into Central California over the route which Walker had pioneered a decade before, a journey of a thousand miles in country through which nothing larger than a horse or slower than a man had ever been taken.

Joseph Reddeford Walker was now forty-four. He had been born in Virginia just before his family moved west to Tennessee. In 1832 he had gone to work for Captain Bonneville as his chief lieutenant in an effort to compete with the American, Hudson's Bay and Rocky Mountain Fur companies. Bonneville sent Walker from the Green River rendezvous to explore the Great Salt Lake and country beyond, country never before seen by a white man, and instructed him to try to make his way to California to find new sources of fur. The clerk of the expedition said of Joseph Walker that:

"To explore unknown regions was his chief delight."

Now, in 1843, Walker led his caravan around the north side of the Great Salt Lake to the Mary's River, westward to the Sink, then due south to Walker Lake, after which he cut west into California and followed the barren, terror-striking eastern slope of the Sierra Nevada where it is said even of the Indians that in order to survive a man must be able to sleep in the shadow of his arrow. After traveling the base of the mountains for days, and hauling his party up the rocky slopes to Owens Lake, Walker now feared for the very existence of the people under his care. He ordered the first immigrant wagons to enter California to be abandoned, burying the parts of Joseph B. Chiles's mill in the sands of the Owens Valley desert, not to be found again until some miners accidentally unearthed them twenty-five years later.

At last on Christmas Day the party found what they described as "a little paradise" at the headwaters of a tributary of the Salinas River, with grass and game and water. They descended into the Salinas Valley, found their way to the Gilroy rancho, delegated Walker to secure their passports, then scattered throughout central and northern California.

About October 20 Chiles and his party of nine men had reached Goose Lake in the northeast corner of California, moved rapidly down the Pit River to the Sacramento River and by November 10 were in Sutter's Fort, having pioneered a new and relatively safe route to California . . . but not for wagons, any more than Walker had found his eastern slope of the Sierra Nevada navigable for the big slow, heavy, clumsy land schooners.

That stupendous drama was still a few years in the future.

CHAPTER XV

The Men Match the Mountains

TWO MORNINGS AFTER CHRISTMAS, Lieutenant John C. Fremont stood on the southern border of Oregon. To the east lay the Oregon Trail and a quick, safe journey homeward; to the south lay the unexplored deserts and mountains of what is now western Nevada. His party of twenty-five men had been away from home for nine months, they were hungry, many of their pack animals had died or been stolen by Indians; all of their topographical orders had been carried out. If he turned homeward, his job as cartographer would be brilliantly completed.

But New Year's Day of 1844 found him slogging southward through harsh, cutting, black volcanic rock. He was a man of savage insistence, as well as a sensitive poet.

"We continued down the valley, between a dry-looking black ridge on the left and a more snowy and high one on the right. Our road was bad along the bottom, being broken by gullies and impeded by sage. The soil in many places consists of a fine powdery sand, covered with a saline efflorescence, and the general character of the country's desert."

The next two weeks were spent in this frightening deathlike country until the party reached a thirty-five-mile-long lake which Fremont called Pyramid Lake, and from which his men gorged themselves on salmon trout. On this newly garnered strength they pushed through to the present site of Reno, and south of that to Carson River, once again suffering from empty innards and rock-torn feet: probably the lowest point of their morale.

Fremont, who had the gift for histrionics as well as heroics, chose this moment to tell his tattered troop that they were going to force a crossing of the Sierra Nevada westward to the Sacramento Valley. The men had only to raise their eyes to see what Allan Nevins, Fremont's biographer, so graphically describes as:

"This mighty range, in places fourteen thousand feet high, rising precipitously from the east, steep on steep, to the point where, in January, all is silent frozen waste of snow and rock, as bleak, empty, and bitter as the Himalayas themselves."

No white man and probably no Indian had ever crossed the Sierra Nevada in the depth of its winter, a fact which Fremont very well knew.

Not a man demurred; Kit Carson would have guided Fremont to hell and back, had his friend said it must be done. On January 19 they plunged boldly into the mountains. As they came into Antelope Valley, beyond which the ice barrier of the main range shot upward through the sky, friendly Indians warned them not to attempt the crossing. The snow was impassable.

Impassable and impossible, these were fighting words in the lexicon of John Fremont. On February 2 he gave the order to start upward. As though he did not have trouble enough, he was still dragging the army howitzer! His instruments told him that only seventy miles directly west lay Sutter's Fort.

It was to prove one of the longest seventy miles in the history of exploration: within two days the trail that the men were hacking out was strewn with packs and personal possessions. Even the animals could go no farther. An old Indian warned them:

"Rock upon rock, snow upon snow; even if you get over the snow, you will not be able to get down the mountains."

Their last Indian guide deserted. It became clear to Fremont that he could not take his train through until he had found a trail and a pass. The next morning, leaving behind all of the party except Kit Carson and Broken Hand Fitzpatrick, these three indestructible ones went reconnoitering on snowshoes, crossed an open basin in subfreezing cold, moved relentlessly upward for about ten miles against icy barricades.

The men matched the mountains.

Through sheer will power they forced their way. Finally:

"Far below us, dimmed by the distance, was a large snowless valley, bounded on the western side, at a distance of about a hundred miles, by a low range of mountains which Carson recognized with delight as the mountains bordering on the coast."

In the lesser distance was Marsh's Mount Diablo. When Carson saw it he exclaimed:

"There is the little mountain. It is fifteen years since I saw it; but I am just as sure as if I had seen it yesterday."

It took twenty days to bring the animals and supplies up to the peak. The men suffered from snow blindness, from the exhaustion of carving a road out of icy mountains, from such starvation that, inured to a lifetime of hardship as they were, they were reduced to eating their pet dog, Klamath.

One month from the day of the first attack on the salient, Fremont and Carson led the emaciated expedition through to the Sacramento Valley and Sutter's Fort, "two human skeletons wearing Scotch caps."

He had made the first winter crossing of the Sierra Nevada. His only loss was the cannon, which not even the army had been able to get him to abandon; it had had to be left behind in the snows.

John Fremont's forcing of the Sierra Nevada was more than an act of individual heroism; it was a kinetic moment in history, moving the young lieutenant and his country toward what they both thought of as their "manifest destiny." What Fremont could do with an exhausted, unprovisioned band of volunteer voyageurs, the United States Army could do any time it wished! The mountains were no longer insuperable. The last barrier had been breached.

And, for the first time since Commodore Jones had come ashore at Monterey in October of 1842 to accept the premature surrender of the Far West, the United States armed forces were represented on California soil.

Captain John Sutter immediately set about provisioning the twenty-five men, supplying them not only with food but with cattle and fresh mounts, horseshoes, bridles, pack saddles. He made a present to Fremont of a beautiful white horse called Sacramento.

Fremont could allow himself and his men only two weeks of rest; he was in California without passport or permit, and word had been brought that Governor Micheltorena was sending his military commander, Jose Castro, to the fort to investigate Fremont's reason for being there.

John Fremont was only three hundred miles more illegal at this point than he had been when he stepped across the Oregon border into Nevada: according to the maps of the time, California extended eastward at least halfway through present Colorado. In fact, as three California historians have pointed out, Underhill, Goodwin and Scherer, *California and the entire Far West were one and the same.*

"This 'island' of California had no eastern boundary until the California government set it up in 1849. Though California was roughly thought of as extending to or through the Sierra Nevada, actually that natural boundary was not a legal, mapped, or designated boundary. The Fremont-Preuss map of '48 includes most of the Far West in the California area, and at the Constitutional Convention at Monterey in 1849 there was a strong movement, almost successful, to include all of Nevada and a sufficient portion of Utah to include Salt Lake and the twenty thousand Mormons living in the Salt Lake Valley. Actually California extended to the very foothills of the Rocky Mountains...."

Fremont's official instructions were to map and explore. The western-expansionist group had urged him to learn how large an American force would be needed to capture the country. He discreetly stayed away from the California coastline, about which the Mexican authorities were sensitive, and made his way south along the western base of the Sierra Nevada. An Indian guide told him of an unused pass, the Tehachapi. On approximately April 1, 1844, he and his troop once again crossed the mountains, this time heading eastward.

The next time he would move into California with a well-armed band of sixty-five to seventy trained men, to play a stormy, disputed, decisive role in its conquest.

Chapter XVI

Larkin Becomes Consul with a Gold-headed Cane

WITHIN A MATTER OF HOURS after Fremont's party raised its last cloud as it left the eastern Sierra and moved out into the sand and sage flats of Nevada there arrived in Monterey an official document naming Thomas O. Larkin as United States consul in California. This was the first acknowledgment on the part of the United States that there was a government existing in California; and more important, that anything going on in that aboriginal region could conceivably require the presence of an American official, though the British had named James Forbes to be their consul at San Jose in 1844, and a little later the French instructed one of their officials to proceed to Monterey and open an office of the French government there.

April 2, 1844, was the proudest day of Thomas O. Larkin's life; he was convinced that now, with the government in his hands, he could in time effect a peaceable transition to American ownership. He so deeply loved his job that, although the spending of money was to him an exquisite mixture of pleasure and pain, he nonetheless wrote to his friend Alfred Robinson, in New York, asking Robinson to order him a resplendent uniform with gold epaulets. Apparently he did not stipulate what kind of uniform, there being none for a consul; just any handsome uniform would do. The symbol of authority in California had always been a cane, and Robinson, who dearly loved a practical joke, ordered Consul Larkin two canes with solid gold heads, the bill for which elicited screams of mortal agony that could be heard all the way from Monterey to New York.

Consul Larkin's duty was to represent the United States in all the land between the Pacific coast and the Rocky Mountains, the southern border of Oregon and San Diego. While his chief task was to facilitate trade he soon found himself officiating at marriages and funerals of the Protestant residents, sitting as judge over quarrels between Americans on ships on the high seas. His immediate duty became the caring for sick sailors off American vessels, many of whom he took into his own home, literally feeding them out of his own pocket. When their number grew too large he built the first hospital in California. His major difficulty was that there were no doctors available.

Dr. John Marsh's informal entry into the profession without benefit of the Hippocratic Oath had been followed by two more practitioners: Joe Meek, a colorful Rocky Mountain character, said to his companions while coming down from Oregon with an emigrant train in 1843:

"Boys, when I get down among the greasers, I'm going to be a doctor."

Though Meek could neither read nor write, his friends promptly called him "Doctor" Meek, and when he reached Monterey he found a following: for in one of his first cases, that of a Mexican boy who had cut off his toe with an ax, Meek stuck the boy's toe back on with mud, and it grew.

The second to enter the field was G. M. de Sandels Waseurtz, who wrote a colorful description of his journey through California in 1842 and 1843. Waseurtz was a mining engineer who visited with John Sutter in 1843, studied the countryside, and informed his totally disbelieving host, who had long ago heard the Indian's tale of Coloma's Lake of Gold ruled over by a carnivorous monster, that there was unquestionably gold in the region of the Sacramento. He then went on to Monterey, which he described as "not yet grown out of its quilts, though the inhabitants, both Creole and foreigners, are a very kind, hospitable, and merry sort." Here, because of his botanizing and mineralizing, the rumor got around that Waseurtz was a "medico."

"I had studied the Materia Medica, I could look grave and wanted business, so I became a doctor. I laid down some broad principles, one was to charge well, the other, never to prescribe anything that was not disagreeable to take."

The California Medical Association now consisted of "Doctor" John Marsh, "Doctor" Joe Meek, and "Doctor" G.M. Waseurtz, all of them charging high prices and apparently only mildly impeding nature in its cures.

By one of the ironic coincidences which turns history into fascinating melodrama, at the same moment that Thomas O. Larkin became United States consul for California, Governor Micheltorena issued the most forward-looking set of ordinances the long-neglected territory had known since the progressive regime of the Spanish Governor Borica in 1800. He ordered the establishment of the first public school system in the Far West, with schools at San Diego, Los Angeles, Santa Barbara, San Jose, Yerba Buena and Sonoma. Attendance was compulsory for both sexes between the ages of six and eleven, the parents to be fined in case of absence; the teachers' salaries were set at $480 a year. He passed laws regulating excessive medical fees, declared Yerba Buena an official port of entry, where foreign ships could pay fair landing fees and duties, and tried to put an end to smuggling and the bribery of Mexican officials. He also returned the missions to the padres, though for exclusively religious purposes, in an effort to stop the beautiful buildings from falling into utter ruin.

Micheltorena is the last of the Mexican governors to play an important part in the pageant of the Far West. He was probably the handsomest man to enter California, tall, slender, with a warm personality in spite of a military bearing, gray kindly eyes, light complexion and brown hair; wealthy, well read, well disposed to all the people under him. Had the Mexican government been seriously interested in retaining California, had it provided Micheltorena with an army of one hundred well-armed, trained soldiers instead of convicts and marauders, the conquest of the Far West might have changed radically in character.

In honor of becoming an official port, and Governor Micheltorena's appropriating the sum of $800 for the building of a customs house, the fifty residents clustered along the little cove of Yerba Buena petitioned to become a pueblo or town. By 1844 Yerba Buena had only a dozen houses. It was not merely the cold fog, nor was it the lack of vessels coming through the strait; more and more whaling vessels were anchoring in the bay though they preferred the north side of the strait where there was good water, abundant wood, proximity to the ranchos and fresh food. Nor was it that the inhabitants were too somber, for Marsh in an irascible moment described their chief activity as:

"Getting drunk and running up and down hills."

Richard Henry Dana, in a book called *Two Years Before the Mast*, recently published in Boston, was saying:

"The Californians are an idle, thriftless people, and can make nothing for themselves. The country abounds in grapes, yet they buy bad wine made in Boston, and buy shoes made of their own hides and carried twice around the Horn."

Somehow the town had not caught on: it had become mainly a trading outpost for the Hudson's Bay Company, which American and European settlers did not enjoy. The Mission Dolores, four to five miles out from the cove, was falling into ruins, the presidio overlooking the strait, built by the Spaniards in 1776, had been pilfered almost down to its foundation by people wanting free adobe brick and lumber for their own buildings.

It was not a bad place in which to settle; there were wild strawberry patches on the hills out toward the ocean, and each spring when the berries ripened families would come in from as far south as San Jose, and Sonoma to the north, and the entire town of Yerba Buena would pack its blankets and cooking apparatus and move out onto the dunes for a week of picnicking and dancing and whatever entertainment could be provided by the officers of the ships in port. Down the peninsula there was good horseback riding and hunting for deer and bear. On the same block in which William Rae had his headquarters for the Hudson's Bay Company (he and his wife and daughter lived behind the store), there was a public house with a billiard room and bar owned by Jean Vioget, a Swiss, where the single men of the town gathered in the evenings to be joined by captains and supercargoes for heated political arguments on the relative merits of James K. Polk and Henry Clay for the presidency.

A trading ship fitted up below deck with counters full of merchandise, as though it were a shop in Boston, would sell between $15,000 and $20,000 worth of goods in a three-to four-week stay, receiving in payment hides, tallow, sea and land otterskins, beaver skins, some few Spanish or Mexican doubloons, the residents of Yerba Buena and the ranchos taking home with them the highly prized sugar, tea, coffee, clothing, blankets, jewelry and rich cloths for the making of beautiful gowns.

Yet nobody wanted to settle in Yerba Buena, no one from the Emmons Party from Oregon, the Bidwell Party from Missouri, the Workman-Rowland Party from Santa Fe, the Joseph Chiles and Joseph Walker Party. The tiny mud and adobe hamlet was the ugly duckling of the Far West.

CHAPTER XVII

Seed Wheat of the Western Migration

TOWARD THE END OF AUGUST there moved majestically into the northeast corner of Nevada, coming southwest from Fort Hall, the only overland party of 1844 headed for California. The Stevens Party proved to be the archetype of all emigrant parties, seed wheat of the westward migration.

Each emigrant train has an individuality and life cycle comparable to that of a human being: conception, birth, youth, maturity, death, dissolution and immortality . . . bestowed by biographers.

The conception of the Stevens Party was similar to other emigrant trains, accidental and consisting of strange elements. The leader was probably the ugliest man to cross the plains: Elisha Stevens, about forty years old, born in South Carolina of a French Huguenot family, was raised in Georgia, became a blacksmith by trade but spent most of his adult years as a hunter and trapper in the Northwest. He is described by the members of the party as courteous but silent to the point of taciturnity, a lean turkey-necked man with a long, narrow, misshapen head and a huge beaked nose which looked like a caricature of an eagle. He came alone to the meeting place on the Missouri River (later called Council Bluffs) in the early spring of 1844 with a well-built wagon and animals fitted for the trail, without knowing whether there would be a group heading west, and bumped into a party of fifty men, women and children who, although total strangers to Stevens, concluded after a few days that:

"He was born to command."

The largest individual segment of the Stevens Party was the twenty-member Murphy clan led by Martin Murphy, who had been born in Ireland, emigrated to Canada looking for more political freedom, and from there to Missouri. In Missouri the family had been plagued by malaria; there were no schools or churches. After the death of his wife, Martin Murphy met a Catholic missionary who told him about California, where good health and religion were abundant. As to the location of this wonderful land, the missionary knew only that it was on the shore of the Pacific Ocean, that it lay in a westerly direction from fever-stricken Missouri; as to the distance or route or character of the country, he had no knowledge. Yet every member of the Murphy family agreed wholeheartedly that, come spring, they should move out for California.

The second largest segment of the party was the Townsend and Montgomery group, who were friends and neighbors in Missouri, numbering seven.

Though the coming together of the leader and the two major groups of the party was accidental, there was nothing of chance about the fastidious preparation that preceded their departure from Council Bluffs on May 18. There were eleven wagons in the train, all good farm wagons, some built for the specific purpose of crossing the continent, drawn by good oxen and accompanied by many horses and a large herd of cattle. The success or failure, the amount of suffering and tragedy to be encountered is dependent upon the organic structure of each party: the ratio of old men and young children to those in the prime decades of life; the trades and skills that are represented; the ability of the members not only to choose wisely in their leader, but to submerge differences of racial origin, religion, economic and cultural backgrounds in the interests of the whole train. The Stevens Party had an authentic medical man along, a Dr. Townsend; it had a blacksmith and a gunsmith; there were three men with mountain experience, in addition to Caleb Greenwood, who had been picked up as a guide, his two half-breed sons and three French Canadians who had had backwoods experience.

Four of the twenty-six men could be considered old, there were three youths of seventeen and eight boys ranging in age from three to thirteen. The other twenty men of the party ranged from John Sullivan at twenty up to Stevens at forty, all at the height of their physical powers. The women too were of a favorable age for such a long and dangerous journey: of the eight, five were wives under thirty-six. There were one widow and two unmarried girls. The main body of the party was composed of successful families who had been able to purchase the best equipment and put in supplies to last for eight months.

The Murphys, Townsends and Montgomerys, though they had the votes to elect anyone of their choice, indulged in no such prideful egoism; they fixed upon Elisha Stevens and gave him their confidence. Therein lies their genius as a party; in this lack was born the tragedy of the Donner Party: between their extremes of total fulfillment and total tragedy fall all the hundreds of emigrant trains that filled the prairies and mountains in the second migration decade from 1849 to 1859 in the most fabulous westward trek the world has ever known.

The first third of the Stevens journey was uneventful; from Fort Hall the party followed the Walker wagon trail of the previous year down the Mary's River to the Sink, which it reached on October 1. On this date the Stevens Party sat around its campfire to make a fateful decision: to follow the Walker tracks which led south even though there was no way to know whether the Walker Party had been successful; or to push directly west into the mountains, for which a majority voted. At that moment an old Indian, talking to Caleb Greenwood by means of signs and diagrams drawn on the dusty floor of the Nevada desert, told of a river some fifty miles directly west across the desert in the mountains, which flowed down the east side of the Sierra Nevada; by following this river to the crest, he claimed, they could descend into California.

Captain Elisha Stevens with Dr. Townsend, Joseph Foster and Truckee the Indian set out to determine whether the river was there, and whether it could be ascended. They returned three days later to report that they had found the river, with good trees and grass, and that there probably was a pass somewhere beyond it in the mountains.

The Stevens Party took time to cook two days rations, to fill all available receptacles with water and to prepare its wagons, then made a forced march of thirty-six hours to Boiling Springs on the desert, and another twelve-hour march which brought it to the river. Resting for two days to refresh the cattle, the party began the ascent of the river, named it Truckee after the Indian guide, flourished on the plenitude of food, water, grass and game.

After a few days the ranges began to pack closer, the country became rough, wagons and animals had to be led up the bed of the stream, which was so crooked that in one day it had to be crossed ten separate times. The first snowfall buried all grass.

"The poor footsore oxen, after toiling all day, would stand and bawl for food all night in so piteous a manner that the emigrants would forget their own misery in their pity for the cattle."

After weeks of winding up canyons the party reached the fertile grasslands of a meadow surrounded by pine-covered mountains, then moved through the heavily forested country to an icy lake. Ahead stood a great wall of granite domes.

Here again Stevens went out with the best of his men to scout the towering peaks, finding a narrow, winding trail which he believed was a break in the range, and which could take them over the summit.

The tremendous mountains discouraged Dr. Townsend, who was bringing in a wagonload of merchandise to be offered for sale in California. Moses Schallenberger, Dr. Townsend's seventeen-year-old adopted son, agreed to remain on the lake and build a cabin for comfort, hunting and passing an adventuresome winter. In the spring Dr. Townsend would come back with oxen and they could take in the salable merchandise without risk. Two other young men, Joseph Foster and Allen Montgomery, offered to stay with the lad.

On the face of the great mountain two feet of snow had already fallen. The wagons had to be unloaded, the contents carried on the backs of the men, the teams doubled or trebled to haul the empty wagons. Halfway up the mountain the Stevens Party met a vertical cliff, solidly blocking the trail. Inch-by-inch searching revealed a narrow crevice by means of which a man could painstakingly lead the oxen one at a time up through the face of the rock.

Then, at the bottom, chains were fastened to the tongue of a wagon, the cattle at the top hitched to the chains, the men at the bottom pushing and straining and shoving the wagons, the animals hauling from above. Every last wagon was successfully brought up the face of the formidable rock. Once again the men had matched the mountains.

A twenty-five-mile push westward brought them to the headwaters of the Yuba River. Here a number of the families settled down with their wagons to wait for the end of the hard snows. Many of the able-bodied men started down the side of the mountain, reaching Sutter's Fort between the tenth and thirteenth of December 1844.

Back at the lake the three young men protecting Dr. Townsend's wagon faced a winter of starvation, the heavy snows making hunting impossible. Fashioning crude snowshoes, they set out to cross the mountains. Foster and Montgomery made it, Moses Schallenberger became ill, turned back to a winter alone in the desolate cabin.

The remainder of the Stevens Party descended the mountains into the California valley in good health and good spirits, their wagons and equipment intact. John Bidwell and Chiles-Walker, who had attempted to bring wagons through, had lost their possessions en route. The Stevens Party not only opened the last third of the California Trail but proved to be the forerunner of the colorful covered-wagon era just ahead.

CHAPTER XVIII

A Democratic Army, Out for No Good

THERE WAS LITTLE OF cruelty in the nature of the Californios; in their internecine quarrels they dueled with pointed proclamations rather than swords. Aside from hunting grizzly bears and wild horses, their sport was largely confined to incredible feats of horsemanship; they were reputed to be the greatest since Genghis Khan, so skillful that they could pick up a kernel of corn from the earth, coming at full speed.

When in July 1844 word was received in Monterey from the Minister of War in Mexico City that war would be declared as soon as the United States Senate ratified the treaty annexing Texas, and that a citizens' army must be rallied for the defense of Mexico, the long-suffering Californios decided not to recruit, but rather to get rid of Micheltorena's convict troops, who had been despoiling their fair country. Alvarado and his military commander, Castro, warned Micheltorena to ship his soldiers back to Mexico; when Micheltorena refused on the ground that bad troops were better than none, Alvarado and Castro rounded up a force of forty to fifty followers. Not a shot was fired nor a blow struck, despite the fact that the opposing men rode and maneuvered for two weeks. Nor is it likely that anything more untoward would have happened had it not been for John Sutter, who came riding onto the scene on his white charger.

On July 21, 1844, Governor Micheltorena had appointed Sutter captain of all the troops of the Sacramento Valley; and at long last Sutter's fiction of having been a captain was turned into a resplendent truth. It was a heady realization for the man; no accomplishment of his life gave him more prideful pleasure. It also came close to being the death of him.

The appointment did not catch Sutter unprepared. His fort had been organized on a military basis from the beginning, with drill every evening after supper, his Indians wearing the uniforms with red trimmings which came with the purchase of Fort Ross, goose-stepping to barked German or Swiss commands of one of Sutter's drill sergeants, carrying on their shoulders the Fort Ross flintlocks which Napoleon had reputedly left behind in his retreat from Moscow.

In October Sutter learned of the impending revolt of Alvarado and Castro against Micheltorena. Sutter brought the warning to Governor Micheltorena who, delighted at this unexpected support, gave Sutter a formal dinner, sent up a balloon for entertainment, promised Sutter not only more leagues of land for himself in northern California but the legal right to make land grants to all men who would fight under Sutter's command.

Even as Sutter returned to his fort to organize a brigade, Alvarado and Castro captured Micheltorena's few artillery pieces at San Juan, where Micheltorena had moved his troops. Micheltorena signed a treaty agreeing to send his soldiers back to Mexico, which satisfied Alvarado, Castro and even Vallejo, who had remained neutral but urgently wanted the convict army out of the country.

But Captain John Sutter was not giving up so easily what might easily be the only war of his lifetime. He sent out calls to every man in the valley to join his troop, drilled the entire population of his fort; even ordered John Marsh, on pain of military arrest, to join his army as a foot soldier.

Without Sutter's support, Micheltorena would have been obliged to send his cholos back to Mexico as he had agreed to do; with Sutter ready to put almost a hundred armed men into the field, Micheltorena reasoned that he had the strongest army in California. He ordered Sutter to capture Alvarado and Castro. Sutter tried to get a hundred horses from Vallejo for the campaign, but received instead as brilliant and passionate a series of letters as have been written on California soil, in which Mariano Vallejo, the wisest and ablest of all the Californios, made a number of trenchant points which should have put an end to Sutter's folly. Vallejo had discharged his garrison at the end of 1844 on the grounds that he could no longer support the troop of thirty soldiers, thus removing himself, as he had in Alvarado's uprising in 1836, and in the arrest and deportation of Graham and his followers in 1840, from the internecine wars.

It was at this point that twenty men of the Stevens Party dropped into Sutter's Fort, looking for a chance to get a good start in California. Sutter showed them his official document from Governor Micheltorena promising free and legal land, perhaps a league in length, to each man who fought against what Sutter claimed was a group of upstart rebels. The opportunity was too good to miss; every man, including Elisha Stevens and Dr. Townsend, agreed to go to the wars.

At dawn of New Year's Day, 1845, the now Colonel John Sutter rode forth to glory wearing "a tilted cap, a blue frock coat, immaculate trousers, polished boots, a moustache and a marked military air." Behind him was his Army of the Sacramento, approximately two hundred twenty men, the Sacramento settlers, the fresh recruits from the Stevens Party, a hundred Indians. About half the men were mounted; at the rear came Sutter's artillery and his supply wagons pulled by oxen.

It was a thoroughly democratic army, out for no good.

The fort was left in charge of Pierson B. Reading, fifteen whites and thirty Indians, a dangerous procedure, but Sutter seemed more concerned about his favorite common-law wife than his fort, for he wrote to Reading:

"In case I should be killed, you will see that Manaiki receives her wages coming to her until the last day of her being at the establishment."

It was dashing red-cheeked Colonel Sutter's plan to meet the ninety-man army of Alvarado and Castro at San Jose and overcome them in a decisive battle. By January 9 he had joined Micheltorena's forces at the Salinas River. But Alvarado and Castro had no intention of accommodating Sutter's quick plan for conquest; they began moving southward. The heavy rains of the central California valley began making mud baths of the roads. Micheltorena fell ill and had to travel in a carriage. The army moved only four miles a day, provisions gave out, the men were cold and drenched. At this point Marsh, enjoying his revenge, began to ask the Americans why they were getting involved in somebody else's family argument. No one had an answer.

Yet Sutter managed to hold them together, slogging their way southward to Santa Barbara, living off the cattle they could find along the way, foraging at the missions, then down the coast for several more weeks, until on February 19, after seven weeks away from home, Sutter's army made its way to the oak-studded desert plain of the San Fernando Valley and saw the rebel army.

Alvarado and Castro had gone to Los Angeles and convinced that somnolent community that Sutter and his foreigners were going to burn Los Angeles to the ground. They enlisted the help of most of the local Americans, including such old residents as Abel Stearns, the men who had come across with the Workman-Rowland Party and forty recently arrived American mountaineers.

On the morning of February 20 Colonel Sutter ordered his three artillery pieces to begin firing. He was answered by Alvarado's and Castro's two cannons in a barrage which lasted for a couple of hours, after which Castro withdrew his troops westward through Cahuenga Pass. The next morning Colonel Sutter's troops found to their astonishment that the opposing troops were not Californios but Americans, among them old friends from Missouri and Santa Fe.

Private John Marsh took over command from John Sutter, signaling for a truce. The two groups of Americans came together with exclamations of joy and demands for news of friends and relatives back home. Marsh made a speech convincing both sides that they had no place in this war but should rather save themselves for the real contest which would make California American. The Americans left the field of battle arm in arm.

That was the end of the war. Historians cannot agree on the casualties; they range from one horse to four. All authorities agree on the loss of one of Castro's cannon wheels.

Colonel John Augustus Sutter, of the Sacramento Army, Retired, was captured, stripped of his uniform, jailed. The irate Angelenos who blamed him for the foolish fracas disagreed on only one point: should he be shot or hanged for his crime?

Sutter wrote an abject letter to the new governor, Pio Pico, putting the blame on former Governor Micheltorena: Was he not simply following inescapable orders? Pio Pico and the amiable Alvarado not only pardoned Sutter, allowing him to keep his fort and his empire, but confirmed the grant of three additional leagues of land nine miles wide by a hundred miles long promised him by Micheltorena if he would fight. They also confirmed the land grants he had promised to the Americans and Europeans who had joined his army. Everyone was happy, even Micheltorena, who was tired of California and wanted to get back to Mexico City.

Meanwhile William Rae, head of the Hudson's Bay Company in Yerba Buena, earned for himself the dubious distinction of becoming California's first suicide, an act which his contemporaries agreed was due to a combination of business difficulties and getting caught with his inamorata. Because of this tragedy the Hudson's Bay Company decided to shut up shop in Yerba Buena. John Sutter had one less creditor on his neck, but the future of the town of Yerba Buena looked gloomier than ever.

When, two years later, the British lost California partly because they had no representation there, they could console themselves by blaming the loss on a woman.

John Sutter returned to find his fort and affairs badly neglected. Nevertheless he immediately dispatched Caleb Greenwood to Fort Hall to divert any Oregon-bound caravan to California and Sutter's Fort by means of his pledge to give them free land!

In July of 1845 he welcomed with his usual hospitality the Clyman-McMahon Party of thirty-nine men, a widow, and her three children, down from Oregon. Green McMahon, who had first come into California in 1841 with the Bidwell Party, had led them on a thirty-one-day voyage down a chain of rivers: the Klamath, Shasta and Sacramento. The international flavor of the Far West settlement was in evidence, for the party included a Frenchman, a Canadian, two Germans, the others being British and American. Equally varied were its crafts: there were a soapmaker and a chandler, a saddler and a tailor, a blacksmith, a shoemaker, five carpenters, a sailor, twenty four farmers; James Clyman, who kept a diary of the journey and hence got his name attached to the party, James W. Marshall, a coachmaker and a number of mountain men.

Chapter XIX

The Rugged Individualist Train

I N COLORADO FIVE COMPANIES of United States Dragoons, two hundred fifty to three hundred strong, led by Colonel Stephen Watts Kearny, were the first troops to enter any part of the Far West since Captain Zebulon Pike in 1806 and Colonel Stephen Long in 1820. About July 10 Kearny brought his mounted infantrymen into Colorado from Wyoming where he had supposedly been protecting the emigrants on the Oregon Trail from Indian attack. Since the Oregon trains had been going through in safety for several years now, the Kearny expedition obviously had another purpose. Kearny swung down sharply to Bent's Fort, immediately across the line from Mexico's southwest territory, where he enjoyed what the Bent's Fort's biographer described as "a lavish dinner spread in the big apartment," while he discussed Mexico's military strength with Charles Bent, as a prelude to his commanding, the following year, the Army of the West.

Stephen Watts Kearny was descended on his mother's side from such wealthy and socially elite Dutch families as the Van Cortlandts and Schuylers. His paternal great-grandfather came from Ireland in 1704; his father became a prosperous wine merchant in Perth Amboy, New Jersey, then lost everything because he supported the British cause in the War of the Revolution. No one ever doubted Stephen's loyalty. He entered Columbia College in 1811 at the age of seventeen, but left to join the army at the beginning of the War of 1812, and in the course of one year had distinguished himself for bravery, been wounded, captured, exchanged and made a captain. Army life was to his liking. At the close of the war he was sent on expeditions to the frontier to build outposts and forts, to command Fort Crawford at Prairie du Chien in 1828, where John Marsh had had him arrested for illegal use of stolen lumber, and for resisting civil authority.

Now fifty years old, Colonel Kearny was an experienced frontiersman, but a plodding, routine commanding officer who had seen no warfare for thirty-three years.

Kearny and his dragoons stayed in Colorado three weeks before heading east again about August 1, probably passing on the trail Captain John C. Fremont's Third Expedition, consisting of sixty mountain men, which reached Bent's Fort on August 2. Fremont's party included Joseph Walker, Basil Lajeunesse, the experienced hunter Lucien Maxwell, Edward M. Kern of Philadelphia, an artist, and a dozen Delaware scouts who were fanatically loyal to Fremont. Fremont sent a message to his friend Kit Carson, who was ranching on the Cimarron. When Carson learned that Fremont had been ordered to explore a route through the central Rockies of Colorado, as well as to map the Great Salt Lake, he promptly sold his ranch and joined the expedition.

Fremont spent two weeks at Bent's Fort, then with twelve new carbines which he would give as prizes for marksmanship set out for Pueblo where they camped on August 20, continuing up the Arkansas Valley in fine, late summer weather, enjoying the pine woods and the Rocky Mountain streams of southern Colorado and following an old Indian trail which Pike had used in 1804 but which no one had evaluated for the possibility of emigrant trains.

At this same time there came into Nevada four emigrant groups variously known as the Snyder-Blackburn, the Swasey-Todd, the Sublette and the Grigsby-Ide, all part of the same train of a hundred wagons which had assembled in Missouri over a period of several weeks. Only fifteen wagons were going to California; the rest were headed for Oregon.

They were, that is, until they got to Fort Hall where Caleb Greenwood and his sons were waiting for them with Sutter's promise of free land in California. The leader of the party made a passionate speech to hold his train together; he forbade any wagons that had agreed to go to Oregon to turn off on the California Trail under the threat of being held mutinous.

The threat did no good. Greenwood convinced as many as sixty wagons with over a hundred people to turn south at the beginning of the California Trail.

The first party to strike off was led by one of Greenwood's sons, and consisted of twelve young men on horseback with pack animals. They traveled quickly across Nevada to the Mary's River, down to its Sink and then over the trail blazed by Stevens the year before, dropping into Sutter's Fort at the end of September, the fastest crossing in the history of western expansion, with no untoward incident except that young John Greenwood, the half-breed, managed to shoot and kill an Indian.

The Grigsby-Ide Party was the largest to hold together as a unit, consisting of fifty men, besides the women and children. William B. Ide had been a teacher when he was not well enough to practice his trade of carpenter. He is best known as the leader of this party, not because he made the most important contribution but because he was a good writer who left a vivid account for ravenous biographers to absorb. Ide, who was born in Rutland, Massachusetts, in 1796, very early fell victim to western fever and moved first to Kentucky, then to Ohio, then to Illinois. He could not resist the call of this ultimate West, and so over the winter of 1845 he carefully selected the timbers for two of his three wagons, had them made to order with the canvas covers sewed by Mrs. Ide and their seventeen-year-old daughter Sarah. Ide painted the bed of the wagon and the canvas a slate gray, installed cooking utensils and provisions to last six months, in addition to a circular saw and some mill-irons with which to begin life in the Far West; he also rounded up a hundred sixty-five cattle and twenty-eight work oxen. On the back curtain of his hindmost wagon he painted in bold black letters, OREGON. Caleb Greenwood changed his mind.

Once the Ide Party was in Nevada their guide, "Doctor" Joe Meek, whose medical practice in Monterey apparently had fallen off, told them there was no longer any danger from the Indians. The party abandoned the central discipline which had characterized all trains up to this time, each family camping separately at night.

Facing Nevada Mountain, Ide found several level spaces between the cliff ascents where teams, if led up one by one, could stand and haul up the wagons by pulley and tackle. He persuaded the group to work together, to empty their wagons while the men carved out a road six or seven feet wide, cutting down trees and hauling rocks out of the way. When the road was ready, each ox was led up the cliff by ropes; when five or six oxen had been assembled at the first level, each wagon was hauled up the side of the cliff: each wagon up one hitch, block the wheels, beak the teams, take another hitch, move forward a few feet, block the wheels. Within forty-eight hours the entire train had reached the summit, the men exhausted and the oxen bleeding. But they were ready to begin their descent.

With the conquest of Nevada Mountain all remaining cohesion vanished, every wagon dashing ahead to be the first to arrive, and to get the best free land, by its actions earning the title of The Rugged Individualist Train of 1845.

John Sutter wrote in high glee to Thomas Larkin at the beginning of October, enclosing a list of the emigrants:

"It will no doubt be gratifying to you to learn that they are in better condition than any other emigrants who have ever come to this country. They are generally well provided with all the necessary articles useful in keeping house, farming, and also in a number of mechanical branches. The majority of them are also provided with money to a greater or lesser extent."

Apparently California was attracting a better class of emigrant.

By October 10, 1845, when the first of the Grigsby-Ide Party had already pulled its wagons inside the main gate of Sutter's Fort, Fremont's expedition reached fresh-water Utah Lake. They fed well on deer, elk and a stray herd of buffalo which they were surprised to find so far west, and on buffalo fish named from the hump on its back. Traveling northward, Fremont learned that he had made an error in connecting Utah Lake with the Great Salt Lake; he spent two full weeks on the shores of the Salt Lake sketching and making maps. Now a couple of hundred miles south of the regular Mary's River trail, Fremont wanted to head directly west.

"The route I wished to take lay over a flat plain covered with sagebrush. The country looked dry and of my own men none knew anything of it. The Indians declared to us that no one had ever been known to cross the plain."

Carson says of this desert in his autobiography:

"It had never before been crossed by white men. I was often here. Old trappers would speak of the impossibility of crossing, that water could not be found, grass for the animals, there was none. Fremont was bound to cross. Nothing was impossible for him to perform if required in his explorations."

Fortunately, Fremont had ingenuity to match his courage.

"Nearly upon the line of our intended travel, apparently fifty to sixty miles away, was a peak-shaped mountain. This looked to me to be fertile. I arranged that Carson, Archambeau and Maxwell should set out at night, taking with them a pack-mule with water and provisions, and make for the mountain, I to follow with the party the next day and make one camp out into the desert. They to make a signal by smoke in case water should be found."

Fremont and the main body of men set out late the next afternoon and traveled all night. Before morning Archamheau came riding back with the happy news that he and Carson had found water, grass and wood at the foot of the mountain. Another stretch of westering desert had been conquered.

Fremont's Third Expedition had come straight across Utah and Nevada from the Great Salt Lake and proved that all the maps up to this point, which had shown this basin to be "a sandy, barren plain without water or grass," were wrong; it was not one vast desert, but was "traversed by parallel ranges of mountains, their summits white with snow while below, the valleys had none. Instead of a barren country, the mountains were covered with grasses of the best quality, wooded with several varieties of trees, and containing more deer and mountain sheep than we had seen in any previous part of our voyage."

Fremont elatedly renamed the three-hundred-mile-long Mary's River, which became known as the "Highroad of the West," the Humboldt River, after his idol, the German naturalist geographer Alexander Humboldt.

On December 10 he made an easy descent into Sutter's Fort by way of Walker's Lake. This time he did not leave California; he remained, indirectly causing the seizure of the Far West, the war in California, and the setting up of the first American government. He thereby earned for himself either fame or infamy, depending on which book you read: for biography is a disputatious art.

Among the rugged individualists of the Grigsby-Ide train Fremont would find many kindred spirits who, the following year, would be at the heart of the Bear Flag Revolt.

CHAPTER XX

"Why is Captain Fremont here?"

EIGHTEEN FORTY-SIX was the year of resolution for California. Mariano Vallejo of Sonoma had written to Mexico City on November 22, 1845:

"The emigration of North Americans to California today forms an unbroken line of wagons from the United States clear to this Department, and how can they be turned back without forces and resources? It is necessary, sir, it is indispensable that the Supreme Government should send us both. This has been for some years my incessant supplication. Troops and money! Only by uniting both can they save us from the imminent danger that surrounds us. It would be very desirable to close that door of communication between the United States and this country, even at some sacrifice. Castro having made propositions to Sutter for the purchase of his establishment, he said that he would cede it to the government for one hundred thousand dollars. I grant that this is a very high price to pay for a few pieces of cannon, a not very scientifically constructed bastion, some moats, ten or twelve adobe houses, and corrals of the same material; but the security of the country is what is to be paid for, and that is priceless."

The question of the security of Mariano Vallejo's country was eliciting a good many other letters.

Merchant Thomas O. Larkin, who at the beginning of 1846 would transfer the management of his mercantile business in Monterey to a young associate, Talbot H. Green, so that Consul Thomas O. Larkin could devote full time to the acquisition of California for the United States, had written to Secretary of State James Buchanan:

"The Mexican troops about to invade the province have been sent for this purpose at the instigation of the British government."

Secretary of State Buchanan's reply, written in Washington on October 17, 1845, is imperative to the understanding of Captain Fremont's uprising in California and of the misbegotten war with Mexico:

"The future destiny of that Country is a subject of anxious solicitude for the Government and people of the United States. The interests of our Commerce and our Whale fisheries on the Pacific Ocean, demand that you should exert the greatest vigilance in discovering and defeating any attempts which may be made by Foreign Governments to acquire control over that Country. In the contest between Mexico and California we can take no part, unless the former should commence hostilities against the United States; but should California assert and maintain her independence, we shall render her all the kind offices in our power as a Sister Republic. Great Britain by the acquisition of California would sow the seeds of future war and disaster for herself; because there is no political truth more certain than that this fine Province could not long be held in vassalage by any European Power. The emigration to it of people from the United States would soon render this impossible."

By the end of January 1846, Fremont arrived in Monterey with eight of his men for a visit with Consul Larkin. Colonel Alvarado and Prefect Manuel Castro at Monterey, alarmed at this conjoining of officials of the United States Departments of State and War, sent a polite but firm inquiry to Consul Larkin: "Why is an American army officer in California with a body of troops, and why is Captain Fremont in Monterey?"

Captain Fremont, a man of charm, appeared before the officials and with the utmost tact replied that his followers were not soldiers, but mountain men helping him to survey and map a tenable route to the Pacific, that he had left the main body of his men "on the frontier," that as soon as his group had recouped its strength, and he had laid in supplies he would leave California for Oregon, and then home. The meeting was friendly.

Then there occurred one of those fateful accidents which etch the external pattern of events. When Fremont told Alvarado and Castro that he was in California on an exploring expedition, and that he had left the main body of his men "on the frontier," he was telling a half-truth. Even so he was doing better than Secretary of State Buchanan, whose letter was filled with quarter-truths. The main body of Fremont's men were in the mountains, but he had not left them there: they were lost. While still in the Nevada desert, he had sent forty-four of his voyageurs southward under Joseph Walker to enter California by the pass discovered by Walker in 1832, then to make their way down the San Joaquin Valley to the Kings River. Walker had waited instead at the fork of the Kern River. Scouting to find out where his commander was, Walker located him near San Jose, and by mid-February brought his men to join him.

Captain Fremont now had with him a band of sixty armed, devoted and disciplined riflemen, the most effective military force California had ever seen. Had Walker taken his men north to Sutter's as planned, Fremont, accompanied by only eight men, would have returned to Sutter's. But with his entire troop assembled, waiting for advice that the United States was at war with Mexico over the annexation of Texas, Captain Fremont was reluctant to take his force far from Monterey where he expected to raise the American flag.

He reached the coast near Santa Cruz, and the same kind of weather that had bogged down Sutter's army the year before gave him his excuse to stay. By March 1 he headed south along the coast toward Monterey, encamping at the Alisal ranch of the Englishman William Hartnell in the Salinas Valley. He could no longer effectively claim that he was exploring. Fremont wrote Larkin that he was going to remain in the Salinas Valley until spring when, he was certain from everything that had been told him in Washington, the war would have commenced.

The Mexican officials had to confront Fremont or lose face. On March 5, 1846, the near-shooting war over California began.

"In the afternoon the quiet of the camp was disturbed by the sudden appearance of a cavalry officer," wrote Fremont. "Lieutenant Chavez seemed disposed to be somewhat rude and abrupt. This one brought me peremptory letters from the general and prefect, ordering me forthwith out of the department, threatening force in the event that I should not instantly comply with the order. I expressed to the envoy my astonishment.... And I desired him to say in reply to General Castro that I peremptorily refused compliance to an order insulting to my government and myself."

The intensity of Fremont's explosion was probably sparked by his sense of guilt; an opportunist himself, he was the perfect selection to carry out the opportunistic policy of his government. The next morning he "moved up the mountain and encamped on a small wooded flat at the top of a neighboring eminence, Hawk's Peak in the Gavilan Mountains," built a log fort and raised the American flag.

It was now three and a half years since Commodore Thomas Ap Jones had raised the American flag at Monterey in his thirty-hour acquisition of California; both outbursts were indicative of the trigger-happy frame of mind to which the United States Departments of State and War had fanned their officers.

Fremont, from the top of his mountain, could see Mexican troops assembling at San Juan with artillery. He wrote as charming a gasconade as ever came from the gifted Mexican authorities: "If we are attacked we will fight to extremity, and refuse quarter, trusting to our country to avenge our death. If we are hemmed in and assaulted here [he had established his camp with a perfect escape hatch down the rear of the mountains!], we will die, every man of us, under the flag of our country."

On the second evening a troop of Mexican cavalry came part way up the mountain. Fremont took forty men down the mountain to a concealed thicket to meet them. Happily, no one fired a shot, and both parties returned to their camps; Colonel Castro to issue a proclamation charging that "a band of robbers commanded by a captain of the United States army . . . sallies forth making scandalous skirmishes."

The word "robbers" was occasioned by the accusation that Fremont's men had stolen some horses; the phrase "scandalous skirmishes" by the charge that a couple of Fremont's mountain men had burst into a ranch house and frightened three young Californio girls.

The next day when the sapling holding aloft the American flag fell down, Fremont issued a proclamation that the falling of the pole was an omen that their stay in the fort on Hawk's Peak should be concluded.

Thus the army was no more successful than the navy in making the conquest stick. In the contest of international good manners, the Mexican officials won an indisputable victory.

While Captain Fremont took his men slowly, reluctantly northward to Sutter's Fort and then up the American River toward Oregon, a meeting took place in Consul Larkin's drawing room that is perhaps the most illuminating in the Mexican ownership of California. The subject under discussion was:

To whom should California and the lands of the Far West belong?

General Castro declared for annexation to France for religious reasons. David Spence and William Hartnell spoke in favor of their native England. Thomas O. Larkin and Victor Proudon favored the United States. Colonel Mariano Vallejo made a scholarly speech explaining the Constitution of the United States, "and how under it California would have representation in Congress as well as any other state of the republic."

Rafael Gonzales provided the fireworks, springing to his feet from the Larkin sofa with the ringing words: "*California libre, soberance, y independiente!* California free, sovereign and independent!"

No one went on record as favoring, or believing remotely possible, any continued allegiance to Mexico!

CHAPTER XXI

Confidential Agent

O N APRIL 17, 1846, six months to the day after he had received his secret orders from Secretary of State Buchanan, there appeared in Monterey a lieutenant of the United States Marines who had made his way across Mexico from Vera Cruz to Mazatlan, then by the U.S.S. *Cyane* to Honolulu and to Monterey. His name was Archibald Gillespie; he purported to be either a merchant in pursuit of business or a semi-invalid in pursuit of health. A more explosively healthy marine officer has never lived; sending him in disguise to California with dispatches for Consul Larkin and Captain Fremont was as subtle as it would have been to send the U.S.S. *Cyane* into Monterey Harbor with its forward guns firing. On the previous October 30, President Polk had written in his diary:

"I held a confidential conversation with Gillespie of the Marine Corps about eight o'clock p.m. on the subject of the secret mission on which he was about to go to California. His secret instructions and the letter to Mr. Larkin, United States consul at Monterey, in the Department of State, will explain the object of his mission."

Polk discreetly refrained from confiding to his diary the content of the secret orders; Gillespie with equal discretion never set them down in writing. Before reaching Vera Cruz, Gillespie committed to memory all dispatches from Buchanan intended for Consul Larkin, carrying across Mexico only his letter of introduction to Larkin and family letters to Captain Fremont.

Lieutenant Gillespie was warmly received by Larkin, who had been advised of his coming in a letter from Secretary of State Buchanan which set forth the plan as hatched in Washington:

"In addition to your Consular functions, the President has thought proper to appoint you a Confidential Agent in California. You will take care not to awaken the jealousy of the French and English Agents there by assuming any other than your consular character. Lieutenant Archibald H. Gillespie of the Marine Corps is a Gentleman in whom the President reposes entire confidence. He has seen these instructions and will cooperate as a confidential agent with you, in carrying them into execution."

Lieutenant Gillespie apparently brought news of an April war with Mexico, for Larkin, after hearing Gillespie's secret instructions, had the temerity to tell

Vallejo that the United States flag would be flying over California by the Fourth of July!

Consul Larkin now entered the conspiracy by writing a double talk letter to Vice-Consul Leidesdorff of Yerba Buena in which he said that Gillespie:

"Has not enjoyed good health and wishes to travel through your part of California to enjoy the climate."

He told Leidesdorff to provide Gillespie with boat, horses, men, to be charged to Larkin, then added that Gillespie "is a Gentleman of much information, and well acquainted with the countries he has passed through."

He also provided Gillespie with letters of introduction to Americans and Europeans whom he believed were anxiously awaiting conquest: Nathan Spear, important merchant of Yerba Buena, Jacob Leese, Dr. John Marsh, William Richardson, captain of the Yerba Buena port, and John C. Sutter. This last proved a mistake, for peripatetic Sutter reported to General Castro, when Gillespie came up the Sacramento River looking for Fremont, that he was sure Gillespie lied when he told the people he was traveling for his health:

"I have seen his name in a list of officers. It is my opinion that Gillespie is a courier for Captain Fremont . . . with important dispatches from his government . . . and it may be that Fremont will return from the frontier."

Important naval officers on the Pacific had apparently also been advised that war would start in April. When Commodore Sloat, a cautious commander, heard of Captain Fremont's stand at Hawk's Peak he sent Commander Montgomery of the U.S.S. *Portsmouth* from Mazatlan to Monterey with orders to break all records in getting there. Commander Montgomery told Consul Larkin that in his opinion, "Commodore Sloat may by the next mail have a declaration on the part of the United States against Mexico."

Up the Sacramento, Sutter quite plainly told Gillespie that he knew he was an active officer for the United States; but that did not prevent him from providing Gillespie with his best mule and guide. With the help of experienced settlers Lassen, Stepp, and Neal, Gillespie again set off. It took him eleven hard pushing days during which his group suffered near starvation and threats from hostile Indians before he met with Fremont at Klamath Lake just north of the California border. Gillespie delivered to Captain Fremont letters from his wife, from his father-in-law, Senator Thomas Hart Benton; and oral accounting of the confidential letter of Secretary Buchanan to Consul Larkin; President Polk's secret instructions; and the immediate news that the U.S. warship *Portsmouth* was in San Francisco Bay.

Gillespie may also have communicated to Fremont the message from Secretary of the Navy Bancroft which Bancroft later testified he had sent to Fremont:

"Being absolved from any duty as an explorer, Captain Fremont was left to his duty as an officer in the service of the United States, with the further authoritative knowledge that the government intended to take possession of California."

Fremont's letters from his wife and Senator Benton, couched in the cryptic language peculiar to intimates who have discussed a subject thoroughly over a period of years, appeared to Fremont to urge him to play the leader's role in acquiring the Far West for the United States.

"I saw the way opening clear before me," said Fremont. "War with Mexico was inevitable; and a grand opportunity now presented itself to realize in their fullest extent the far-sighted views of Senator Benton, and make the Pacific Ocean the western boundary of the United States. I resolved to return forthwith to the Sacramento Valley in order to bring to bear all the influences I could command."

By the end of May Fremont and Gillespie had made their way down the Sacramento Valley, camping at Lassen's rancho, and the farm of Neal and Dutton on Deer Creek. Both men were exhausted by the forced march and diet of horse meat, but they were prepared for immediate action. Gillespie left on Sutter's launch for San Francisco Bay and the U.S.S. *Portsmouth* with a requisition from Fremont for guns, ammunition, money, food, medical supplies. As an army officer Fremont had no right to requisition navy supplies; if Commander Montgomery honored the order it would appear that he had orders to do so.

The Americans in central California were excited by the return of Fremont: it could only mean that Gillespie had brought him instructions to take California. Despite the fact that the sorely tried Californios had behaved with exemplary kindness to the Americans, a cold war of propaganda was flashed from rancho to rancho with the speed of the swiftest horses: General Castro had been to Sonoma to secure horses and men and was about to attack in force.... Mexican troops would arrest all Americans, take away their lands, deport them eastward over the Sierra Nevada.... Mexico had sold California to England.... British warships were en route to San Francisco Bay.... Mexico was granting three thousand square leagues of land to Father Eugene McNamara, an Irish colonizer, for which he was bringing over three thousand families to settle in California and vote California into the British Empire....

Believing that delay might mean the loss of California to England, that if they did not strike fast and hard, Mexican troops would attack and capture them, the Americans in the Sacramento, Napa and Sonoma valleys decided to rise in armed rebellion.

To their astonishment Fremont refused to ride out at their head as their commanding officer: it had been made clear to him that the United States did not wish to appear predatory. However he left no doubt that although he must remain in the background he would support and sustain them in their uprising. He chose for what he called his "field lieutenant" a tall, spare, rawboned trapper named Ezekiel Merritt, whom Fremont called "fearless and simple." In the forenoon of June 9 Merritt set forth from Fremont's camp with eleven or twelve emigrants and hunters, of a class which Fremont describes as "having nothing to risk." The next morning Merritt surprised Arce, General Castro's secretary and militia lieutenant. Arce was properly indignant at having been surprised, and hence cheated of the opportunity to fight. Lieutenant Merritt offered to repeat the maneuver, *sans surprise*. A more amiable solution was reached when Merritt gave Arce and his men back their guns and their private horses, keeping the military supplies.

Merritt returned to Fremont's camp, increased his band to thirty-three men and, on Fremont's orders, headed southwest through the Napa and Santa Rosa valleys, picking up American volunteers on the way. Their instructions were to capture Colonel Vallejo's garrison, seize all the arms and take command of Sonoma.

At dawn on June 14, Mariano Vallejo was awakened from sleep by the sound of gun butts rapping the big front door. He had reason to sleep soundly, for he was the single most successful rancher in all of central California: he owned leagues of land, his herds were increasing and he was building a library he loved deeply. In order to stay out of the intra-governmental quarrels between General Jose Castro and Governor Pio Pico he had dismissed the last of his remaining troops; the barracks on the north corner of the plaza were deserted. Vallejo was so disinterested in the mounting tempers between the Californios and the Americans that when he went to sleep he left on guard two aged Indians and an old dog, all of them sleeping as soundly as their master when Ezekiel Merritt's men came down from the hills and through the plaza.

Vallejo, still in his nightgown and nightcap, went to the window and saw standing in the square a group of men "armed, mounted, fierce-looking," wearing flat coonskin or coyote-skin caps, and others with red bandana handkerchiefs. Dr. Robert Semple, who was one of the leaders, wrote:

"Almost the whole party was dressed in leather hunting-shirts, many of them were greasy; taking the whole party together they were about as rough a looking set of men as one could well imagine. It is not to be wondered at that anyone would feel some dread in falling into their hands."

It is doubtful if Mariano Vallejo had ever felt the emotion of dread; he donned his uniform, went down to the ground floor and ordered the doors opened. Captain Merritt, Robert Semple, William Fallon and Samuel Kelsey came into the big hall. Vallejo asked: "Gentlemen, what is it you would have of me, and who is the leader among you?"

He was told, "We are all leaders here."

Merritt was designated as the spokesman, explaining to Vallejo that the Americans were determined to make California independent, adding:

"Towards you and your family we have no other feeling than regard, though we find ourselves under the necessity of taking you and your family prisoners."

For Vallejo this was by no means a surprising or unhappy moment; it had been his conviction since 1840 that California would one day become part of the United States. It was also his conviction that becoming part of the United States was the best thing that could happen for the development of California. If the group of hunters and ranchers standing before him in their buckskin pants and greasy shirts were neither an imposing nor an edifying sight, Mariano Vallejo had read widely enough to know that history is not always made by the washed or the genteel.

By this time Jacob Leese, who was married to Vallejo's sister, had come into the great hall along with Victor Proudon, Vallejo's secretary, and Salvador Vallejo, Mariano's brother. When Merritt demanded immediate surrender of the guns, cannon and powder connected with the former garrison, Colonel Vallejo turned them over and then suggested that they sit down at his table in the sala and draw up the articles of capitulation, asking only that life and property be carefully guarded. Vallejo assumed that the group was acting under the orders and supervision of United States Army Captain John C. Fremont; although he had never met Fremont, this fact gave him assurance that everything would be done in an official and decorous manner.

Vallejo's excellent *aguardiente* proved a trifle strong for the empty stomachs of the negotiators, who had not the slightest idea of what should go into the treaty. After being joined by John Grigsby, and then William B. Ide, of the Grigsby-Ide Party, Vallejo completed the drawing up of his paper of capitulation, which apparently he did without intervention from the Americans around the table; for in this, his last official paper, Colonel Vallejo was still trying to play the part of the conscientious Mexican officer who had been overwhelmed by a superior force.

When the paper was read aloud to the men outside, dissension broke out among the Americans. Grigsby, who had understood he was working under Captain Fremont, stepped down from leadership when he realized that this was a freebooting movement. Loquacious, excitable, spluttering Ide took over command. There was strong dissent against releasing the Vallejo family, Leese, Proudon and the other Sonomans on their word of honor not to take up arms.

Vallejo, who had expressed the hope that Captain Fremont would come immediately to Sonoma and set up American headquarters there, was not disturbed when informed that he and his brother, and Proudon, were to be taken to Fremont's camp under arrest. Since his friendship for all Americans in California was of such long standing, he assumed that he and Captain John C. Fremont would shake hands, then Vallejo would express his pleasure that California was at last to become part of the United States; that he would thereupon be paroled or invited to join the American forces. He assured his wife, Benicia, that he would be back in a few days.

It had been a peaceable revolution. No one had been hurt, no property had been disturbed. The only breach of decorum was that the *aguardiente* Vallejo had sent out to the men in the plaza made them a little noisy.

With the departure of Vallejo from Sonoma, the California Republic was formally born. The Americans decided that they must have a flag and William Todd, nephew of Mary Todd Lincoln, set out to design one. Mrs. Elliott cut a piece of white cloth from a bolt of cotton she had in her home, a red stripe for the bottom was provided by Mrs. Josefa Mathews, while paint was secured from the Vallejo home. The Americans wanted a star on their flag to tie them into the tradition of Texas; this was put in the upper left-hand corner, then to the right young Todd tried to draw a California grizzly bear. He was not a very good artist, and the bear came out looking like what the amused natives of Sonoma called a pig. Underneath the star and the bear there was printed in crude lettering:

CALIFORNIA REPUBLIC

Probably at dawn of June 15, 1846, the day following the seizure of Sonoma, the Bear Flag was raised.

CHAPTER XXII

Paradise Grows a Trifle Ugly

WHILE WAITING FOR NEWS of Merritt's band, John Fremont moved down to Sutter's landing with a few picked men, leaving his main body up on the American fork. Here he learned that Gillespie had returned from the *Portsmouth* and that three officers from the *Portsmouth* had been sent to assist him: the purser with some bags of American coin to help finance operations, Lieutenant Hunter in charge of the launch, and a Dr. Duvan "to arrange my medicine chest and to render any assistance in his power," suggesting that Commander Montgomery anticipated a certain amount of fighting.

The arrival of cash, supplies and officers from the United States warship Fremont interpreted to mean that the navy was under orders to render him full cooperation, that from this point forward the conquest would be a joint army and navy operation. If any further corroboration was needed by Fremont it was contained in Commander Montgomery's letter:

"I am also informed by Lieutenant G. of your having expressed to him a desire for the presence of a vessel of war at Santa Barbara; if you shall still think that the presence of a ship of war at Santa Barbara may prove serviceable to you in carrying out the views of our Government, and will do me the favor to communicate your wishes with information as to the time you will probably reach that part of the coast, I shall not fail (Providence permitting) to meet you there with the *Portsmouth*."

Captain Fremont next sent Kit Carson and a small group of men to Sutter's Fort to demand its surrender. Captain John Sutter was an army officer as well as a civil official of the Mexican government, but his need for military heroics had been satisfied in the civil war the year before. In one vast renunciatory gesture he stripped himself of his captaincy in the Mexican army and control over his fort by throwing open the gates and welcoming Kit Carson as Fremont's emissary. His reign as monarch of the Sacramento Valley, which had begun with his arrival in the wilderness in the fall of 1839, was ended.

Now John Fremont, who knew nothing about Mariano Vallejo except that he was the military commandant of the Mexican forces in the north, sent Vallejo and his party to Sutter's Fort as prisoners. Sutter received them with open-armed hospitality; over the years he and Vallejo had sometimes disagreed, but the two men respected each other. Sutter installed the group in his parlor. Bidwell, who was working as Sutter's secretary, brought them their meals and sat chatting with them while they ate.

Fremont was fighting a war under equivocal conditions; if he played a major role in capturing California for the United States, anything that might be interpreted as an irregular action would be forgiven him; but if he failed. . . He therefore sent his map drawer and artist, Edward Kern (who had been sadly needed in Sonoma two days before to make the California bear look like a grizzly instead of a pig), into Sutter's Fort to take command, and to institute a stricter regime over the prisoners. Vallejo and his group were locked in inadequate quarters, they were allowed no visitors, the food was poor. The days passed, the four or five which Vallejo thought would bring him home, and the weeks passed, and still they were locked in their rooms in the fort.

The harsh treatment of Colonel Vallejo and his family was a breach of etiquette which all too soon gave way to gunshot wounds.

By June 17, when Sonoma had been under the Bear Flag for three days, an alarm was spread throughout the bay area that General Castro of Monterey was advancing on the Sacramento Valley to recapture the seized garrison.

William Ide, still in command at Sonoma, sent two Americans, Fowler and Cowie, northward toward the Russian River to pick up a keg of powder at the Fitch ranch. Since there were in the neighborhood some twenty armed Californios under the command of Juan Padilla waiting to join forces with Castro, the two men were urged not to travel by the main road. Fowler and Cowie were not worried about their opponents; they stayed on the road, were captured by Padilla and executed near Santa Rosa.

Ide sent out a small party to search for Fowler and Cowie; they had a skirmish with Padilla, wounding one of the Californios and capturing another who informed the Sonoma garrison of the shooting of the two men.

With this news the entire tone of the conflict changed; Americans and other foreigners who had wanted no part of the conflict came into Sonoma as volunteers, Grigsby returning to take charge of the rifle company. Families from the surrounding valleys were brought into the garrison for protection. Fremont left Sutter's Fort at the head of his troops, publicly acknowledging leadership of the conquest.

He reached Sonoma on June 25, a hundred sixty men under him. Finding no danger there he headed toward the bay, and in his first service as a military captain was outmaneuvered by de la Torre, a Californio who, needing time to get his men across the rough San Francisco waters, planted a false message to fall into Fremont's hands. Fremont wheeled his force; by the time he learned of the ruse and had returned to San Rafael, de la Torre had moved his troops across the bay. As a retaliatory measure Kit Carson, when he saw three Californio civilians land in a small boat nearby, shot them.

Paradise was growing a trifle ugly.

The poetic Californio officer, Arce, said:

"California is like a pretty girl, everybody wants her."

The courtship was getting rough.

From San Rafael Fremont crossed the bay with his troops, went to Fort Point, the presidio founded by the Spanish. The ancient guns were harmless but he went through the ceremony of spiking them, assisted by Captain William D. Phelps and his crew off the Yankee trading vessel, the *Moscow*, thus getting the merchant marine involved in the uprising.

The Sacramento Valley and all lands north of San Francisco were now in American hands. Captain John C. Fremont, conqueror of central California, sat for his portrait to Captain Phelps:

"Captain Fremont, a slender and well-proportioned man of but pleasing appearance . . . dressed in a blue flannel shirt open at the collar, over a deerskin hunting shirt, blue cloth pantaloons and neat moccasins, all of which had evidently seen hard service: a light color handkerchief bound tightly around his head. A few minutes conversation convinced me that I stood in the presence of the King of the Rocky Mountains."

It was a sentiment the Californios, somewhat naturally, did not share.

Commodore Sloat, aging, conservative officer in charge of the Pacific flotilla, had his orders to help capture California once war with Mexico was declared. Unwilling to repeat the premature flag-raising *faux pas* of Commodore Jones in 1842, Sloat took the half-way measure of sending the U.S.S. *Levant* and the *Cyane* to California, but remained himself in the Mexican port of Mazatlan hoping that each hour would bring him the declaration. At last, without it, he sailed north to Monterey, arriving there on July 2 on the *Savannah*. There had been no Mexican flag flying in Monterey for two months, nor were there any soldiers in the garrison. Governor Pio Pico had established his capital in Los Angeles.

On July 4 Fremont stepped into the plaza of Sonoma, addressed the people and declared martial law. A committee consisting of John Bidwell, William Ide and Pierson B. Reading was directed to draw up a plan of government for Sonoma and northern California. In typical frontier fashion the three could not agree, each writing his own organizational report. Bidwell's was selected as the official one, probably because of its brevity.

Although Commodore Sloat took Fremont's action in stepping forth as the head of the Bear Flag insurgents as meaning that Fremont had specific orders from Washington, it still required strong language from one of his own officers, Captain Mervine of the *Savannah*, to get him to move:

"It is more than your commission is worth to hesitate in this matter!" cried Captain Mervine.

Commodore Sloat and Consul Larkin spent July 6 on board the *Savannah* drawing up proclamations, copies of which were sent to Commander Montgomery on the *Portsmouth* in Yerba Buena.

"I have determined to hoist the flag of the United States at this place tomorrow," wrote Commodore Sloat, "as I would prefer being sacrificed for doing too much than too little. If you consider you have sufficient force, or if Fremont will join you, you will hoist the flag at Yerba Buena, or at any other place, and take possession of the fort and that portion of the country."

At ten o'clock in the morning of July 7 forceful Captain Mervine

went ashore at the head of two hundred fifty marines. As there were no Mexican officers to surrender the Monterey garrison, the captain led his men up to the customs house and read aloud the declaration saying that California now belonged to the United States. For the third time an American flag was hoisted in the Far West. The marines gave three cheers, the ships multiplied this with a twenty one-gun salute. After several thousand years of belonging to the Indians, two hundred seventy-nine years as a province of Spain, twenty-five years as a Mexican province, and twenty-four days as a Bear Flag Republic, California had now become American.

And just in time. When the English warship H.M.S. *Collingwood*, which had been playing hide-and-seek in Mexican waters, came around the point and Admiral Seymour saw the United States warships in the harbor, with the American flag flying over the town: "The British admiral stamped his foot in rage and flung his hat upon the deck."

Two days later, July 9, 1846, Commander Montgomery took seventy men ashore at Yerba Buena, marched them to the public square, read the proclamation and raised a second American flag. Lieutenant Revere of the *Portsmouth* had left his ship at two that morning with a third flag and copy of the proclamation, riding at top speed to Sonoma where the flag was raised in the plaza sometime after noon.

To oppose the Americans there were, between Yerba Buena and San Diego, two potential forces: General Castro and Governor Pico in Los Angeles. If these two ranking Californio officers were to combine forces they could give Fremont a fight, but under no consideration could they have waged a serious contest with the marines and four United States ships of war in the harbors: the U.S.S. *Savannah*, of fifty-four guns, the sloops of war *Cyane* and *Levant*, of twenty-four guns each, the frigate *Congress* with sixty thirty-two-pounder long guns.

On July 19, no word having yet been received of a declaration of war, Commodore Sloat met with John Fremont in Sloat's cabin aboard the *Savannah*. The scene was volatile and angry. Commodore Sloat expressed himself as horrified that Fremont should have acted without official U. S. Army orders. At that moment the U.S.S. *Congress* came into Monterey Harbor, Commodore Stockton commanding. Stockton not only approved what Fremont had done, but greatly admired his course of action.

Feeling put upon, Commodore Sloat learned with profound relief that Commodore Stockton, young, vigorous, adventuresome was willing to accept full responsibility for everything that had happened. Sloat gratefully turned over his command to Stockton and sailed out of the Far West waters, relieved to get out of the unresolved mess with no greater opprobrium than "indecisive."

Commodore R. F. Stockton and John C. Fremont liked each on sight, forming a friendship based on identity of temperament. Stockton raised Fremont's rank to major, Gillespie's to captain, and officially took the California Battalion of volunteers into the navy.

Hoping to end the conflict quickly, Major Fremont moved his battalion to San Diego on ships of war and, on August 1, even as General Kearny was leaving Bent's Fort on his way west with his army, Commodore Stockton sailed with three hundred sixty marines and seamen in his flagship *Congress* for San Pedro to effect a meeting with Fremont and subdue southern California, including the new capital at Los Angeles. Consul Thomas O. Larkin sailed with Stockton. Fremont and Stockton believed they would have to defeat General Castro's troops in a major battle in order to put an end to the hostilities, but Consul Larkin, who had been living happily with the Californios for fourteen years, believed that an honorable peace could be negotiated which would enable the Mexican officers to save face and become a willing part of the new American regime.

Larkin nearly succeeded. He wrote to Abel Stearns, who had lived in southern California since 1829, asking him to urge General Castro to send envoys to Commodore Stockton. General Castro assumed that Larkin spoke for the commodore and did so, telling Commodore Stockton:

"Wishing then, with the governor, to avoid all the disasters that follow a war like that which your lordship prepares, it has appeared convenient to the undersigned to send to your lordship a commission...to know the wishes of your lordship....".

All that was required was the kind of gesture that Commander Montgomery was at this time making to Mariano Vallejo, who had been confined in Sutter's Fort for almost a month. Captain Montgomery issued an order for Vallejo's release and, learning that Vallejo was ill, sent Dr. Henderson from the *Portsmouth* to Sonoma to care for him. Although Vallejo had returned home, in his own words to Larkin "half dead," and found that he had lost a thousand cows and horses during his absence, Commander Montgomery's graciousness healed the wounds. Vallejo became an enthusiastic citizen of the new order.

However Commodore Stockton refused to negotiate with General Castro's commissioners; the tone of his reply to Castro offended every Californio. Castro, unable to wage war, and Pico, unable to maintain his government, had little choice but to flee to Mexico.

Two days later, on August 12, official word reached California that the United States and Mexico were at war. The Californios were to rise, in anger and in pride.

CHAPTER XXIII

"There's that damned flag again!"

I F THE SIDE OF COMMODORE STOCKTON that went to war was undemocratic, he made up in part for his unseemly conduct by ordering the first popular elections to be held in the Far West; by asking that California's first newspaper be created for the dissemination of news; by appointing as the first American alcalde or chief magistrate of Monterey and its surrounding territory the Reverend Walter Colton, United States Navy, born in Vermont in 1797, son of a devout father who had served for fifty years as deacon of the Congregational Church. At the age of twenty-one Walter Colton had entered Yale, was ordained at twenty-eight, taught at an academy in Connecticut for four years and then moved to Washington, D.C., as editor and chief writer for the *American Spectator* and *Washington City Chronicle*. For purposes of improving his health he became a chaplain in the navy, toured the Mediterranean for three years and published two volumes of his observations.

Colton had bushy eyebrows and black sideburns that framed normally unattractive features, the nose too bony, the mouth line ragged, but the long, big-domed face was dominated by a pair of burning scholar's eyes.

On Thursday, July 16, 1846, nine days after the American flag had been raised in Monterey, the Reverend Mr. Colton, then forty-nine, came into the thick fog of Monterey Harbor on board the *Congress,* and for the next three years worked wisely and wittily to dispel the fogs obscuring the transition of California to an American possession. Together with Robert Semple, the dentist-printer who had come into California in 1845 with the Hastings party, a man whom Colton in *Three Years in California* describes as "wearing a buckskin dress, a foxskin cap; is true with his rifle, ready with his pen, and quick at his type-case," he created the *Californian,* finding a small press that had been used by a monk for printing religious tracts, using the wrappers of cigars for paper.

Colton could turn a sentence: "Our bay is full of the finest fish, and yet it is rare to meet one on the table. Put a fish on land, and give him the speed of a buck, and he would have a dozen Californians on his trail...." He put out the first edition of his weekly paper on Saturday, August 15, printed in English and Spanish.

As chief magistrate, judging personal quarrels as well as crimes and business disputes, the Reverend Walter Colton gave Monterey its first democratic decisions. Previously, for identical offenses, "The custom had been to fine Spaniards and whip Indians. This discrimination is unjust: I have substituted labor; and now have eight Indians, three Californians and one Englishman at work making adobes."

Colton also introduced modern penology by feeding the prisoners well, paying them one cent an adobe over the required fifty per day, and using no guards. No one ever ran away; if the Indians, given three months for taking another's horse when their own tired, or the Mexicans, given a similar sentence for slaughtering a convenient cow when they got hungry, were puzzled by this sudden change in the concept of private property, they were no more puzzled than was Magistrate Colton when the tangled love affairs of the territory were brought to him for settlement: the case of the Californio girl who, having run away with her lover, but still "as chaste and pure as the driven snow," changed her mind and refused to marry the man. How was bachelor Colton, still remembering the painful time when he had been jilted, to persuade the girl to let him perform the marriage ceremony?

When an important and wealthy Mexican who owed a humble Californio $800 was insulted by the fact that he could be hauled into court by a former servant who could neither read nor write, Magistrate Colton quickly made it clear that the only issue to be discussed was whether or not the don owed the money:

"Law which fails to protect the humble, disgraces the name which it bears."

He confounded two Californios quarreling over a gambling settlement by fining them both; impaneled the first jury ever to sit in California, making it one third Mexican-born, one third California born, and one third American-born, using English-born William Hartnell as interpreter. The people of Monterey were delighted with this newfangled idea, and came to understand what Magistrate Colton meant when he observed:

"If there is anything on earth besides religion for which I would die, it is the right of trial by jury."

If the Reverend Mr. Colton had no competition as a magistrate, it did not take long, only two months, for a competitive newspaper to emerge in Yerba Buena, published by Samuel Brannan, who on July 31 had sailed into San Francisco Bay on the *Brooklyn* out of New York and around the Cape, at the head of some two hundred thirty-eight Latter-day Saints seeking a new home in the Far West. Their purpose in coming to California was to join the main body of their Church, which was moving westward, perhaps to California, no one could be sure. Brannan is said to have exclaimed in disappointment when he sailed into the bay:

"There's that damned flag again!"

Sam Brannan did not possess the self-discipline required of a dedicated Saint; his career in the Church as well as in California was a stormy one. He had been excommunicated a few years before, only to be reprieved by one of the Prophet Joseph Smith's brothers. On his arrival in Yerba Buena he was brought up on charges by his fellow Mormons for misconduct during the voyage. Commander Montgomery presided over the jury trial.

At the beginning of August 1846 there were upwards of two hundred residents in Yerba Buena; when two hundred thirty-eight Saints disembarked, Yerba Buena became, as Bancroft commented, "largely a Mormon town."

Their arrival helped to secure the permanence of Yerba Buena, still being threatened by the possibility of other communities being started on the bay where the ships would be closer to fresh water, food and good anchorage. The hundred-odd Mormon families consisted of able farmers and mechanics who had brought their tools and skills and immediately set to work, some as lumbermen across the strait, which had been named by John Fremont the Golden Gate Strait, others to start a colony called New Hope on the Stanislaus River where they built a barn and mill and cultivated eighty acres in order to have a food supply against the arrival of Brigham Young, who was leading his people out of the bloody battlefield of Nauvoo, Illinois, their sacred city, and across the plains.

There was some fear and suspicion of the Mormons among the Americans in California, yet the people of Yerba Buena made many of the families comfortable in the old mission buildings, while the rest set up a tent colony.

Sam Brannan and his party were not the first Mormons to come into the mountain-banked amphitheater of the Far West. A few months earlier, in the spring of 1846, a party of forty-three Saints traveling in nineteen wagons had left the Mississippi, missed the main body of Mormons moving west, and had struck southward along the eastern foothills of the Rockies with a trader as a guide, finding their way to present-day Pueblo. Welcomed by the small group of Americans and Mexicans living around the adobe post, this vanguard had gratefully built cabins and put in crops while waiting for news of their people. It was the first group since Father Junipero Serra and the mission padres in 1769 to come into the Far West inspired by their religion to seek new frontiers for the purpose of colonizing.

During the winter the colony increased to two hundred seventy-five by the moving in of the sick soldiers of the Mormon Battalion with their families; seven children were born, thought by historians to be the first all-white children to be born in what is present-day Colorado. Yet the colony proved to be temporary, as were the Mormon colonies in Yerba Buena and on the Stanislaus River. The heroic trek and settlement of the main body of the Latter-day Saints in the Far West was still in the future.

Chapter XXIV

Armed Conflict

M OST OF SOUTHERN CALIFORNIA was up in arms. A full-scale revolt had been mounted by the Californios, who had become fighting mad. Their good and sufficient cause was Captain Archibald Gillespie, enjoying his first real taste of power, a man of fertile talent who has been inadequately recognized by history: wherever he passed he dropped the seed of discord, and soon the spot would be blessed by a goodly crop of confusion. Having been made military commander of the southern department and instructed to order martial law in a territory that was largely Mexican, Captain Gillespie became a tyrant over a people who were friendly and, for the most part, persuaded that the Americans would give them a stable government and, since property values in Monterey had increased forty per cent in a few weeks, prosperity as well.

Captain Gillespie knew little about the Californios and liked them even less. With a garrison of fifty men behind him, he became a dictator: no two persons could walk on the streets together; there could be no gatherings in homes, no provision shops open after sundown, no liquor sold without his permission. He shut down their amusements, arrested the leading Californios on frivolous grounds . . . all of which the perplexed but patient people might have withstood had not Gillespie made it all too plain that:

"He looked down on Californios and Mexicans as an inferior race and a cowardly foe."

Four hundred men took up whatever scattered arms were available and, under the leadership of former army officers Captain Jose Flores as comandante general, Jose Carrillo as second and Captain Andres Pico third in command, warmed up for their campaign by besieging and capturing the Chino rancho of Isaac Williams, where twenty Americans and foreigners were under the command of Benjamin Wilson. On September 30 they captured Captain Gillespie and his garrison, Gillespie not even attempting to put up a fight.

The Californios might have been justified in rolling the bumptious Captain Gillespie over a barrel in the plaza; instead they permitted him an honorable surrender, and let him march his men to San Pedro. On October 2 another force of Californios marched on Santa Barbara, but Captain Theodore Talbot, instead of surrendering his small garrison, led it in an escape to the hills while the Californios retook the town.

When word reached Yerba Buena of the uprising in the south, Captain

Mervine and the *Savannah* were sent to San Pedro where Captain Gillespie, on parole not to fight any more, joined Captain Mervine, adding his fifty men to Mervine's three hundred forty. The Californios had dug up an old four-pounder celebration cannon from the plaza in Los Angeles, manufactured some gunpowder at San Gabriel and marched out to meet the Americans, killing six and wounding six others with their cannon fire before the American forces retreated to the harbor and re-embarked on the *Savannah*.

The success of the Mexican victories in the south started guerrilla warfare throughout the state, with bands of Californios capturing Consul Larkin on his way to Yerba Buena, and five sailors at San Mateo; a Californio force under Manuel Castro fought a battle with American troops under Captain Thompson at Natividad, the scene of Isaac Graham's early distillery, with each side losing five or six dead and a like number wounded. Word spread that, aside from the ports which the American warships and their big guns could control, all of California would soon be back in the hands of its former owners.

On October 19 Commodore Stockton sailed from Yerba Buena on the *Congress* for San Pedro to take command, after ordering Major Fremont to recruit in the Sacramento Valley and raise a hundred seventy experienced riflemen. Fremont embarked his men on the U.S.S. *Sterling* for Santa Barbara, whence he was to march south to join Commodore Stockton and recapture Los Angeles. When Fremont reached Santa Barbara he learned of Captain Mervine's defeat, and the fact that the Californios had denuded the intervening country of horses, cattle and supplies. He returned on the same ship with his hundred seventy sharpshooters to Monterey. It was one of the rare instances in his life when Fremont had acted too cautiously, or so Commodore Stockton thought in castigating his friend in a report to the Navy Department. It was another substantial victory for the Californios.

Heading almost straight south along the Rio Grande River was an American armed force under Stephen Watts Kearny. Kearny, who had been made a general for his quick, albeit unopposed subjugation of Santa Fe, had with him a force of three hundred dragoons, about the same force he had brought briefly to Colorado the previous spring. On October 6 General Kearny encountered Kit Carson, who was on his way to Washington with dispatches. Reading Commodore Stockton's proclamation to the effect that California was subdued, General Kearny ordered two hundred of his dragoons back to Santa Fe. He then insisted that Carson give the dispatches to Broken Hand Fitzpatrick for delivery in Washington, and himself guide Kearny to California.

Carson guided Kearny's force further southward, then struck west along the Gila River across present-day Arizona to where the Gila and Colorado rivers join. By crossing the Colorado river, Kearny entered the extreme southeast corner of California. Carson then led him northward to avoid the terrifying desert lying between the mountain range and San Diego. At San Pasqual Kearny was reinforced by Gillespie, sixty mounted riflemen and a third howitzer to join the two cannons the dragoons had dragged all the way from Santa Fe.

On December 6 Kearny's troops came into contact with a smaller force of Andres Pico's mounted guerrillas. Suffering from Gillespie's malady of contempt for the Californios, and failing to obey the elementals of military tactics, Kearny sent an advance guard down a steep hill to charge the Californios, who stood firm, killing Captain Johnson, the commanding officer, and another dragoon. Without order or organization, Kearny's troops now dashed into battle, strung out according to the speed of their horses and mules. Pico, surveying the situation from a knoll, led his eighty men into a charge against the Americans, who were mounted on tired or unbroken horses and intractable mules, much of their flint and powder wet from the rain. The Californios, among the greatest horsemen in the world, had their most effective weapon, their lances, ready.

The result was one of the worst military defeats for an American force since the War of 1812: twenty-one killed, including a number of officers, nineteen wounded, including General Kearny and Captain Gillespie, the loss of a howitzer. The Californios suffered minor injuries.

A relief party sent through the lines to San Diego was captured by the Californios, who again outmaneuvered General Kearny at the San Bernardino ranch. A second rescue party consisting of Kit Carson, Edward Beale and an Indian boy managed by magnificent woodcraft and endurance to get through the lines to San Diego. On December 11 a large force of marines and sailors rescued General Kearny. The next day, December 12, Kearny marched his force into San Diego to combine with Commodore Stockton's men.

If the combined American forces meant big trouble for the Californios, and the war was just about over, trouble for the American commanders was just beginning.

John C. Fremont, who had learned before leaving Monterey with his enlarged battalion, now numbering over four hundred armed and mounted riflemen, that President Polk had appointed him a lieutenant colonel, spent Christmas Day of 1846 in the roughest terrain of the Santa Inez Mountains, suffering from cold, wet and exhaustion, with a hundred fifty to two hundred of the horses dying, the men forced to drag their cannons by hand over the steepest stretches. In San Diego the weather was warm, bright, sunny and dry, but General Kearny was none the happier for it. Though his rank as a general was in every way equal to that of Commodore Stockton, and though in any land push such as they were now planning to put down the remaining fragments of the Californio rebellion, an army general should rightly have been in charge, Commodore Stockton had assumed command of the combined forces.

Kearny, rankling over his defeat, the loss of his men and his howitzer, was profoundly resentful. He was determined to take the command away from Commodore Stockton as soon as the Californio forces had been defeated, not merely the military command which he felt his orders entitled him to, but the civil command as well. Therein lay the makings of a monumental quarrel, all of it played on California soil, but magnified by a Washington court-martial until it became a permanent part of the heritage of the Far West: for the civilization of a country is made up not only of its mountains and deserts, fertile valleys, coastline and mineral resources; the character of a country is formed as much by the character of the men who come onto its terrain.

On January 1, 1847, the Californios, realizing that the Americans now had a well-armed force of some five hundred men marching north from San Diego, and that Lieutenant Colonel Fremont was marching south with another four hundred, sent a letter signed by Jose Flores, under the title of governor, suggesting that since the unpleasantries between Mexico and the United States were probably over by now a truce be declared and negotiations begun for peace.

Commodore Stockton again refused. General Kearny asked for and was granted actual command of the troops under Stockton. This time he sent a strong party of skirmishers ahead to protect his two nine-pounders and four field pieces. The Californios charged in force on the American left flank. The troops held. The Californios retreated. This was the Battle of San Gabriel, the first victory for General Kearny.

The next day, halfway between San Gabriel and Los Angeles, the Californio cavalry dashed out of a concealed ravine and attacked the Americans on both flanks. Using Indian warfare techniques, General Kearny formed his troops into a square with the wagons at the center and the guns at the corners. The Californio attacks failed to push the Americans back and, having a limited amount of powder, they retreated northward.

The following day Captain Gillespie raised the American flag in the plaza at Los Angeles where he had been obliged to haul it down some three months before. Two days later, on January 12, Lieutenant Colonel Fremont, who was near the mission of San Fernando, received a message from General Andres Pico, who apparently had no stomach for surrendering to either Commodore Stockton or General Kearny. Fremont granted Pico a friendly and generous peace in which the Californio officers and men could return to their homes with honor and dignity. He also took back General Kearny's howitzer.

John C. Fremont had created much good will: he had kept his California Battalion rigidly in control on its march down from Monterey, for which the Californios respected him; when he had been obliged to take horses and cattle for his men, he had paid for them with government scrip; he had saved the life of Jesus Pico, one of the most influential men in central California; and he had granted the surrendering Californios all the rights enjoyed by Americans.

The next day he marched into Los Angeles in a heavy rain.

"A more ragged, ill-provided, unprepossessing battalion it would have been difficult to imagine, they might have been taken, as one of them remarked, for a tribe of Tartar nomads . . . only their military order and arms made them seem soldiers."

Commodore Stockton so heartily approved the Fremont treaty that he named Fremont governor of California and commander-in-chief of all the forces.

This was the insult supreme to General Kearny, culminating his weeks of frustration since the defeat at San Pasqual. He promptly wrote to Commodore Stockton and Lieutenant Colonel Fremont announcing that he was commander-in-chief in California, that Commodore Stockton was to cease attempting to set up a civil government, and ordering Fremont to perform no act in government without the specific approval of General Kearny. Commodore Stockton replied angrily that the civil government had already been operating for a number of months, that General Kearny had no power here, and that he would send the insolent letter to President Polk and ask for Kearny's recall.

The next morning, January 17, was the fateful day for young Fremont: being summoned to General Kearny's tent, Fremont gave the general his written reply in which he said that he had been mustered into the navy with his battalion under Stockton and felt that he owed his allegiance to Stockton:

"I feel myself, therefore, with great deference to your professional and personal character, constrained to say that, until you and Commodore Stockton adjust between yourselves the question of rank, where I respectfully think the difficulty belongs, I shall have to report and receive orders, as heretofore, from the Commodore."

This was an error in judgment on Fremont's part, though he had something of reason on his side: Stockton's orders from Washington to set up civil government were dated later and were more decisive than Kearny's; Kearny had acknowledged Stockton as commander-in-chief on the march up from San Diego. But Fremont was an army man, he had been an army officer for nine years; he was responsible to the army.

Grim, hard-bitten Kearny, who had spent most of his life on the Indian frontiers, now showed considerable patience and tenderness for young Fremont, whom he had known from the home of Fremont's wife's family in St. Louis and Washington. Kearny quietly advised Fremont to tear up the letter and to put himself under Kearny's orders or he would end his career in the army.

Fremont remained adamant. Kearny sailed for Monterey with his dragoons, where he set himself up as governor of California, a post Fremont was holding in the south. Commodore Shubrick arrived in Monterey, commanding the frigates U.S.S. *Independence* and *Lexington*. Stockton's command was terminated, and with it Fremont's legal right to serve as governor. Commodore Shubrick, seeing General Kearny's orders, declared him to be "head and commander of the troops in California." From this moment the army and navy worked closely together. Fremont made a wild ride to Monterey, quarreled further with Kearny, was refused permission to take his battalion to Mexico for action or to move his original exploring party back to Washington at his own expense.

There was talk in California military circles that Lieutenant Colonel Fremont would be shot for refusing to obey orders. What actually happened was more degrading to a man of Fremont's high spirit and high pride: he was ordered to follow in the dust of General Kearny's dragoons back to Washington as a military prisoner, there to stand court-martial.

CHAPTER XXV

The Furies Pour Their Pent-up Vengeance

ONE GROUP OF MEN, not strictly an emigrant train, had come over the mountains in 1845. Into the gates of Sutter's Fort had ridden Lansford Hastings, who had returned east from California the year before promising that he would lead back a large emigrant party. Hastings had spent the previous winter lecturing in Missouri on the evils of intemperance in order to raise enough money to publish his book, *The Emigrant's Guide to Oregon and California*; fittingly enough the book was full of intemperate judgment and autointoxication. Hastings was an opportunist whom Bidwell, after considerable association, described as a political adventurer. He had hoped to bring so many people into California who would owe him a personal debt of gratitude that through them he would seize California, either to be joined to Texas or to be part of the United States, with himself as governor of the new territory.

Hastings was handsome, strong-faced, quick and intelligent of speech. In Missouri he had assured everyone that he had been over the California Trail, which was a total fiction. He had been able to assemble only twenty-two men by mid-August, twelve of them soon dropping out. Despite the fact that he was several months too late to risk the journey, Hastings had led the horseback party in over the Walker-Stevens, Fremont Trail. It was the only party ever received by genial John Sutter with a severe reprimand: Sutter looked up toward the Sierra Nevada and the December snows and told them that had they been delayed by even one day they would have been cut off and perished in the mountains.

During the last week of April 1846 Lansford Hastings had again left Sutter's Fort to return east, his purpose being to find a faster, more direct route between Sutter's and Fort Bridger in northeastern Utah, and to persuade emigrant trains to accept his leadership and use his route west...at ten dollars a head. With him was a man named Hudspeth, who had been his companion on every trip since the initial one in 1842, Caleb Greenwood and twenty-three others.

During the first week of May a number of emigrant wagons arriving in Missouri at the same time banded together to form trains: the Bryant-Russell Party, the Young and Harlan parties, the Boggs and Aram parties, the Reed-Donner Party. These groups were no longer as compact or distinct as they had been in the days of the Bidwell, Grigsby-Ide or Stevens parties. With two thousand emigrants on the march, and five hundred teams of oxen, mules and horses, the trail from Independence to Fort Bridger had become an almost continuous stream of men, families and wagons.

Pushing ahead rapidly to reach Fort Bridger before the first emigrant trains arrived from the East, Hastings crossed the Sierra Nevada, descended by way of the Truckee River, followed the Humboldt River. At Bishop's Creek he saw the hoofprints of the Fremont Party of 1844, when Carson and Fremont had crossed the salt desert south of the Great Salt Lake. Hastings wanted his party to take this new, shorter route east; Greenwood refused, taking most of the party northeast to Fort Hall. Hastings, Hudspeth and five men mounted on good horses made the crossing in twenty hours.

On July 20 the first party of 1846 emigrants came into the Far West, the Bryant-Russell Party composed of men who had sold their wagons and oxen for mules, guided by Hudspeth. Lansford Hastings led the Young-Harlan Party of a hundred sixty people. Instead of taking them over the route he had just traversed, he guided them through the unknown, precipice-walled Weber Canyon, barely getting the wagons out onto the salt plain. He then rode up to the top of the canyon, stuck a note on top of a bush warning any oncoming parties not to essay the canyon, but to take the cut-off he had used coming east. He then rejoined his party, followed the Bryant-Russell tracks just ahead, circled Great Salt Lake on the south, and crossed the salt desert on Fremont's trail. The party almost perished because of his serious underestimate of the distance to water, the stock dying, the wagons abandoned, the women and children making their way on foot.

At the south end of the Great Salt Lake, Hudspeth had told the Bryant-Russell Party, because of the scarcity of water:

"Put spurs to your mules and ride like hell!"

They rode like hell, making Sutter's by September 1, in time to join Fremont's California Battalion on its way to San Diego.

By October 10 Lansford Hastings brought in the Young-Harlan group. His timing was dangerously close. Once again he was fortunate, his people safe. The Donner Party coming behind them would have no such luck.

Hastings had been able to persuade only three groups that they should abandon the longer but safer Fort Hall-California trail for his own cut-off: the Bryant-Russell group of nine men, the Young-Harlan Party and the Donner Party of twenty wagons and seventy-three people. Jessy Quinn Thornton recorded in his diary at the Little Sandy River, where the Oregon section of the train separated from the Donners:

"The Californians were much elated and in fine spirits, with the prospect of a better and nearer road to the country of their destination. Mrs. George Donner was, however, an exception. She was gloomy, sad, and dispirited in view of the fact that her husband and others could think for a moment of leaving the old road, and confide in the statement of a man of whom they knew nothing, but who was probably some selfish adventurer."

Tamsen Donner, forty-five, former schoolmistress who was carrying books, school supplies and art materials with which to educate her five young daughters in California, was a woman of considerable prescience.

James Clyman, mountain man, who had just come over the salt desert cutoff and up the Wasatch Mountains, talked his heroic heart out trying to dissuade them from taking any part of Lansford Hastings' advice. As Bernard DeVoto recreates the scene in *The Year of Decision: 1846*, Clyman warned this slow-moving train, already late, already depleted by illness, quarrels, blinding sun and dust, to take the well-established trail:

"It is barely possible to get through [before the snows] if you follow it— and it may be impossible if you don't."

The Donner Party's trek to the new frontier was to become "the greatest catastrophe in the opening of the Far West."

The party made up in Springfield, Illinois, not far from the home of Abraham and Mary Lincoln on Eighth Street. They carried a copy of Hastings' *Emigrant's Guide* in their wagon, along with Fremont's *Reports*. There were nine in the Jacob Donner family, seven in the George Donner family and seven in the James F. Reed family, plus eight hired men and one hired girl, neighbors of the Donners and Reeds working their way across the country to start a new life. There were young William Eddy, his wife and two children, the McCutchen family of three, the Widow Murphy, leading five unmarried children, her two married daughters and their families, Irish Patrick Breen, with his wife and seven children, German Lewis Keseberg, with his wife and two small children, the wealthy German Wolfinger family, Charles T. Stanton, and the assorted single men typical of every emigrant train.

Gentle, amiable, wealthy sixty-two-year-old George Donner was perhaps the first of the secure but tired Midwest farmers to head for California and retirement. James F. Reed, forty-six, a dynamic and wealthy furniture manufacturer, had had considerable success as an executive and handler of men. On the morning of August 3 when the party crossed the Bear River into present-day Utah they were led by George Donner, who had been elected captain on July 20, 1846, but it was James Reed who led the thinking when the party received a letter from Lansford Hastings urging them to use his cut-off, and made the decision to take advantage of the four hundred miles shorter route. At the rate the caravan was moving, ten to twelve miles a day, this cut-off could save them a month of hard travel.

It was Reed who replied to Jim Clyman from the vast abyss of his ignorance of the Far West:

"There is a nigher route, and it is no use to take so much of a roundabout course."

As was the universal practice of emigrant trains, the party took a vote. There is no evidence that the women were permitted to participate; responsible for thirty young children, they probably would have agreed with Tamsen Donner and voted not to gamble with the lives of their young. The men declared for Hastings' cut-off. Hastings in his letter had promised to wait for them at Fort Bridger and guide them safely "to the Salt Lake, and then continuing down to the Bay of San Francisco."

A day or two before they reached Fort Bridger they met Joseph Walker, one of the ablest mountain men in North American history, opener of the great paths to the Far West. He urged them vehemently not to take the Hastings cut-off, but to turn north to Fort Hall.

When the party reached Fort Bridger they found that Lansford Hastings had not waited for them. Without a guide, with not one experienced mountain man or plains traveler among them and, with one exception, not even an experienced hunter, they were still determined to save that four hundred miles.

Now three days into the Far West, on August 6, they arrived at the top of Weber Canyon and found the note Hastings had left on a bush, rejecting his own recommended route down the unexplored canyon. The Donner Party settled into camp and sent Reed, Stanton and McCutchen on horseback down the Weber Canyon after Hastings. They needed the time for neither rest nor repairs, they had just taken four days for this purpose at Fort Bridger. Clyman and Walker had warned them that they were already late, yet for five days they waited until James Reed returned, without Hastings, who had refused to leave the party he was with. Reed had come up the Wasatch Mountains from the west, in the general direction indicated by Hastings' hand-pointed directions.

Once again James Reed was the deciding factor, for he had now traveled down the Weber Canyon and up the Wasatch Mountains. He advised the party that the Wasatch was the better, a decision in which his *Palace Car* with its side steps, top deck for beds, built-in stove, private inner compartment, basement floor for storing food, wider and heavier than any covered wagon yet to set forth on the trail, was of crucial importance. For Reed had seen the steep, twisting Weber Canyon in which the walls finally narrowed to precipices on either side of the river, where the wagons of a previous party had had to be lowered by ropes and tackle, one of them smashing to splinters on the rocks below.

And so in mid-August they began their crossing of the mountains, forced to build their own road every desperate mile of the way, cutting through underbrush, through forests of twenty- foot alder and aspen, crossing a creek twice to a mile, filling ravines with tree stumps, drying out swamps. The party was poorly composed for such work, with only twenty able-bodied men in the group. Blisters and tempers rose, quarrels and recriminations. Range after range of unmapped mountains extended ahead. The journey to Great Salt Lake which they had been told would take a week consumed twenty-one days for the distance of thirty-six miles.

By now the party was split into hostile factions. By now it was September 1. They faced the dread-inspiring vast, hot, crystalline, waterless white salt desert...without guide or leader.

Just before entering the "dry drive" the party came upon a board with a written message, parts of which had been torn and scattered. The pieces were brought to Tamsen Donner, who laboriously put them together. It had been written by Lansford Hastings about twenty-one days earlier. It read:

"Two days and two nights of hard driving to reach the next grass and water."

They spent two days resting the animals, cutting grass, cooking, then followed Hastings' trail toward a range of mountains and made the top by late afternoon. Below, as far as the eye could see, lay desert.

The next day their wheels sank into the light salt sand, the merciless sun beat upon them, the oxen faltered. The train spread out, every man for himself, with the heavily laden Reeds and Donners falling behind because their wagons were filled with a fortune in laces and silks and other merchandise to be traded in California. George Donner had $10,000 in bills stitched inside a quilt.

By the end of the third day the entire train faced death, their water gone, oxen dying under their yokes. James Reed left his wagons at noon, on horseback, and by nightfall reached the base of Pilot Peak and the spring Fremont's advance party had located the year before, just inside the border of present-day Nevada. When he rode back to his family, passing the emigrants struggling forward like ghost-white salt figures in the darkness, he found that his cattle had stampeded into the desert and were lost. Reed now had to bury his *Palace Car* with its fortune in goods in the desert and get his family on foot to the spring.

The "dry drive" had been eighty miles instead of forty, had taken six days instead of two; four wagons were abandoned, one of Keseberg's, one of Jacob Donner's, two of Reed's. The wealth of merchandise owned by the Donners and Reeds, which even as a cold business decision should have kept them on the safe California Trail, was totally lost. The desert trail was strewn with mahogany beds, bureaus, rockers, musical instruments, all the tokens of continuity between the old life and the new. The company faced a sheer and doubtful struggle merely to stay alive. But the common suffering of this ordeal by thirst did not draw the exhausted, frightened fragments of the Donner-Reed train together. Instead, it led to further disintegration.

They spent the next full week resting, searching the desert for their lost animals, bringing in food from the abandoned wagons, sending Stanton, a bachelor, and William McCutchen, a family man, ahead to Sutter's in the hope they could bring back relief. Having no choice, they continued to follow Hastings' tracks, only to find that Hastings, still improvising, had declined to take the route over the Ruby Mountains and instead had driven south for three days looking for an easier pass, only to double back. Since he did not warn those to follow, the Donner Party spent another week following the futile trail south and then north.

On September 30 they reached the Humboldt River and joined the California Trail. The last of their companions from Independence, who had gone by the Fort Hall road, had passed this point from thirty-five to forty-five days before, and the Joseph Aram Party of twelve wagons and fifty people were in sight of Johnson's ranch in the Sacramento Valley. Reed's "nigher route" had proved to be desperately longer in time.

Five days later they were again in serious trouble. In a row precipitated by frayed and anxious nerves, James Reed, trying to quiet the popular but hot-tempered John Snyder from quarreling with Milt Elliott over whose team should have precedence in pulling up a hill, was so severely beaten over the head by Snyder's bull whip that he drew his hunting knife and sank it in Synder's chest. Synder died immediately.

The party was totally shattered. One segment wanted Reed executed. Instead he was banished, without gun or food, leaving his sick wife and children unprotected. Split now into warring factions, the train floundered to the Humboldt Sink. They had no knowledge of how to defend themselves against the Indians, who killed or ran off most of the remaining oxen and cattle.

On October 20 they reached the meadows of the eastern base of the Sierra Nevada. Here Stanton, having returned from Sutter's with two Indian guides and seven mules, found them. Sutter's mules were laden with flour and dried beef. There were now only five hard days driving up the Truckee River to the pass. There had been snow, but Stanton, who had risked his life in the return, urged them to "rest, recoup their animals in this meadow." Even heroes can be guilty of bad judgment.

The party rested for five days, then began the ascent of the Sierra Nevada. The vanguard, the Breens, Eddys and Kesebergs, pushed ahead, passed the cabin built by Schallenberger of the Stevens Party in 1844, and made for the pass. On November 1, when they were only three miles from the summit, they lost the trail in five feet of snow. They turned back to the Schallenberger cabin near the lake, where they dug in. The rest of the party, except the slow-moving Donners, came up and camped. The next day the weather was better and the party started once again for the pass, the children being carried by the adults, Stanton making the summit with his Indians to force a new trail through the snow. He returned to find the half-frozen party camped around a fire, urged them to continue upward the last two or three miles that led to the top of the ridge and safety.

They refused. They were cold, tired, they wanted to rest overnight. They did; but the snow began falling. By morning the drifts were ten feet deep. The pass was closed. They fought their way back to the cabin on the lake. As George R. Stewart observes in *Ordeal by Hunger*:

"The trap which closed behind them at Fort Bridger had closed in front."

Any one day would have saved them: one of the four spent resting at Fort Bridger, one of the five spent waiting for Reed to return from his trip to overtake Hastings, one of the seven spent pursuing Hastings' trail south and then north again, one of the five in the Truckee meadows, the last day's refusal to push the final three miles behind Stanton; one day that the devastating snowstorms might have held off. Or any one of the innumerable days spent in quarreling, refusing to help each other, to share food, water, oxen, friendship, leadership.

In the pioneering of a new land not all the emigrants will come equipped with the moral or physical skills to create an Eden. As diverse as were the impulses to pull up roots and possessions to cross deserts and mountains to a new country, equally diverse were the talents and abilities to cope with it.

There were signs of unselfishness and strength: Reed had divided his food when abandoning his wagon; Eddy had lost his wagon and coupled his team to Reed's when Reed had lost his animals; Stanton had returned from Sutter's with help. There was also the cruelest selfishness and violence: the refusal of the camp to lend Eddy a horse to go back and look for the lost and alone Hardkoop, who consequently perished in the desert; Breen's refusal of water to the suffering Eddy children, and Eddy's getting it only by swearing that he would kill anyone who tried to stop him...but not taking any for himself; Walter Herron and James Smith, wanting to buy oxen from the Breens, who had the largest supply of food, had to pledge two animals for one when they reached California. There was the uncontrolled temper of Snyder, quarreling over who should cross a mountain first; Reed's flashing knife; Graves's insistence that Reed be shot for his crime, the pitiful plight of Reed's wife and five children when he was banished.

All this they took into camp with them on the fourth day of November 1846 at the base of the towering snow-covered implacable western Sierra Nevada.

It was not merely the cold, for there was plenty of firewood and, at first, men to cut in; nor was it the hunger and malnutrition, for at first there were a few beeves, oxen, then the remaining few horses, mules and finally dogs. Their inability to accept discipline or leadership, the inter-family hatreds that pursued them right down to their deaths, so that there never was any sharing of food or hope or comfort . . . these caused their slow destruction; these deprived them of their strongest psychological weapon for survival.

If they suffered from bad judgment, they also had bad luck.

Charles Stanton led a party of sixteen men, six women and two Indian guides across the pass, then refused to continue on because he wished to protect Sutter's property, and the mules were exhausted. Eddy offered to reimburse Sutter, crying out that twenty-two human beings were worth more than seven mules, but Stanton remained adamant. Most of the men and women who forced the pass that night later perished; the mules wandered off in the snow and were lost.

A "snowshoe party," consisting of ten men who were physically able to travel, five younger women and two half-grown boys, forced the pass and for six days fought their way against twelve-foot snowdrifts, subzero weather, snow blindness, totally without food. A new storm descended upon them. Stanton, too weak to continue, saved his companions the problem of abandoning him by saying that he would be along later, then died by the side of the trail in lonely dignity.

The rest knew they must perish unless they had something to eat. They discussed drawing lots to see which one should be killed and eaten, but in the end decided to struggle on until someone died.

The first to go was Antonio, the Mexican herdsman, then Uncle Billy Graves, then Patrick Dolan, the bachelor, then thirteen-year-old Lemuel Murphy. Lying at the bottom of a twelve-foot hole of snow, ice water seeping in at the bottom, "they stripped the flesh from the bodies, roasted what they needed to eat and dried the rest for carrying with them."

No one would eat the flesh of a member of his own family.

Lost and kept going only by the unconquerable courage of Eddy, they made their tortured way westward mile by mile. Mrs. Foster had to watch her younger brother Lemuel's heart broiled over the coals and eaten. Later it was Mrs. Fosdick's turn to watch Mrs. Foster cut the heart and liver out of Fosdick's body and broil them over a fire.

"It was the necessity, not the act, that was deplorable."

But for the killing of the two defenseless Indians there was no moral justification, as Eddy and three women, now so close to death they could barely drag their feet over the trail, testified by refusing to touch the flesh.

Of the ten men who started out with the "snowshoe party," five died on the trail, two were killed, and one boy died before the two remaining men, Eddy and Foster, one boy and all five of the women (the female of the species has greater endurance than the male, as countless stories of the opening of the Far West prove) stumbled into Johnson's camp thirty-three days after leaving the lake; a grisly saga that has no counterpart for suffering or for unquenchable courage.

The slow-moving Donners had never caught up with the main body of the train, but stopped five miles east of the lake at Alder Creek, cut off from all contact or cooperation with the main camp. At the lake the cabins were now buried in nine feet of snow so that they were "cold and damp caves." The men had grown too weak to cut firewood, the last of the animals had died, the main food was the hides which had been used as roofing, boiled to a gelatin-like pulp, and bones of animals long since devoured. Mrs. Reed had been in the gravest danger from the loss of her husband and animals, and had five children to feed as well as several dependents. At the Reed cabins the two drivers turned their faces to the wall and died: Baylis Williams, the family protector, later Milt Elliott. Old Mrs. Murphy cut him up and ate him, all except his face.

One of the Keseberg children died, the baby Catherine Pike died, the first Eddy boy died, then Mrs. Eddy, who had put her last piece of bear meat in her husband's pack when he left with the "snowshoe party." The Breens took in Mrs. Reed and her five children, giving them hides and thrice-boiled bones to eat, or they too would have perished. Mrs. Breen secretly gave some of her remaining food to fifteen-year-old Virginia Reed, who had been on the verge of falling into the coma preceding death, thus saving the girl; yet at this point Breen forced Mrs. Reed to pay him the money they owed for cattle he had given the Reeds earlier.

Human character is unendingly contradictory; and interesting.

Relief was at last on its way; a party organized at Sutter's set forth early in February: seven men, all strangers to the Donners, none of them mountain men, forced a crossing in fourteen days of incredible stamina. The "canyons raced with wild rivers"; it was subfreezing cold; every man, on foot, carried on his back a pack of fifty to seventy-five pounds of food. They scaled range after range of the Sierra Nevada, at night huddled around a fire, unable to lie down. Obliged to make a final trailless crossing of the highest peak, had they become lost they would have died in the ice and snow.

But they were great in heart. They triumphed: Ned Coffeemeyer and Joseph Sels, former sailors; Aquilla Glover and Sept Moultry, farmer-emigrants to California in 1846; John and Daniel Rhoads, brothers who had come into California with the Mormons; Reasin "Dan" Tucker, also an emigrant.

The rescuers rested a couple of days, then started back over the wall of snow with three men, four women and seventeen children. John Rhoads offered to carry little Naomi Pike on his back. They could leave no food behind with the fifteen who remained in the camp, or the twelve at Alder Creek: the Donners, the Breens, the Graveses, the sick and the very young children.

The trek began to be a repetition of the "snowshoe party": Mrs. Reed had to send back two of her children who were too weak to travel; Denton, the

Englishman, failed, quietly died wrapped in the quilt left with him by the freezing Dan Tucker; then little Ada Keseberg died. Moultry and Coffeemeyer were supermen, they forged ahead, located packs of beef from a cache and returned as the majority of the children were weakening.

Then into their camp arrived a second rescue mission led by James Reed, who had been banished more than four months before on the desert. He brought word that all of northern California had risen on hearing of the tragedy, and that a strong, well-supplied rescue party was on its way.

The children's party with Moultry and Coffeemeyer made Sutter's safely, while Reed pushed eastward with nine experienced mountain men to the lake. Here they found conditions of indescribable filth, the small children too weak to walk. Those who died had been eaten.

Reed and his men started for the pass with three Donner children, the Reed children, the Breens and the Graveses. Again men carried small children, again they ran into violent storms.

On the mountains they met Eddy and Foster, returning from Sutter's with supplies to save their families. When the two men reached the lake they received bad news. Keseberg confessed to having eaten the last of the Eddy boys after he had died. Old Mrs. Murphy, who had done a heroic job of keeping the young Foster boy alive, cried out in bitterness that one night Keseberg had taken George Foster to bed with him and the next morning the boy was dead. Keseberg had hung the body "in sight, inside the cabin, on the wall," and then had eaten it. Eddy very nearly killed the demented Keseberg.

Eddy now wanted to lead the rest of the party over the mountain, but Tamsen Donner, here at the lake with her three children, had a sick husband five miles back at Alder Creek whom she had promised to "love, honor and obey until death do us part." She refused to leave her dying husband, though he had only a short time to live, kissed her three girls good-by, knowing they would be safe with Eddy, and walked through the trees, back five miles to the east, thinking perhaps of how she had known all this would happen from the very first hour they had set foot on this Far West. She returned to their tent to be with her husband when he died the next day...and to die herself before the next rescue party would get in. They say of you now, Tamsen Donner, more than a hundred years later, that as you walked through the woods to your duty and to your death, leaving behind three young daughters, you never looked back.

The Donner Party has a mystical meaning in the settlement of the Far West: it is Greek tragedy, moving one to pity and terror, the bloodletting par excellence; the ultimate cup of grief into which all of the tears avoided by former parties are shed. All of the bad judgment and bad luck somehow skirted by the others is heaped upon the hapless heads of the one party on which the furies pour their pent-up vengeance at having been cheated of their victims these five long years during which dumb, stumbling men had overcome the unscalable mountains, unendurable salt and sand deserts. It is the ultimate tragedy without which no distant frontier can be conquered; and which gives a structural base of blood and bone and suffering and sacrifice and, in a sense, of redemption, to a new people creating a new life in a new world.

CHAPTER XXVI

A Curse Is Removed, San Francisco Is Born

AT THE OPENING OF 1847 Yerba Buena was still a reluctant lady, unable or unwilling to grow. Perched on a sheltered cove of the bay which sailors for a hundred years had agreed was the greatest harbor on the face of the earth, capable of housing comfortably all of the assembled navies of all the nations, it rarely harbored more than one whaler or trader at a time. There was little reason for merchants to settle here, since there were few ships and fewer people to trade with. The land itself consisted of sand dunes, unfitted for agriculture. There were no ranches. On January 1, 1847, Yerba Buena had about three hundred white residents; of whom two hundred were Mormons, most of whom would depart when the main Mormon Church settled elsewhere. Viewed from a rowboat in the bay, the hamlet showed about fifty houses, wood and adobe dwellings, half a dozen of them two-storied, starting from the sands of the cove and straggling backward up the bleak surrounding hills.

Then, on January 30, Alcalde Washington Bartlett, otherwise known as Lieutenant Bartlett of the U.S.S. *Portsmouth*, decided that there was too much confusion in the fact that the town was known as Yerba Buena by those inside its small environs, but to the rest of California was known as San Francisco because of its mission. Bartlett issued a pronouncement that Yerba Buena would in the future be known as San Francisco, and had the news published in the first newspaper of the town, the *California Star* which Sam Brannan had begun publishing with a press he had brought out to establish a newspaper for the Mormons. Bartlett also named Jasper O'Farrell to survey the city proper, to draw up an official map, to lay out streets, all of them to intersect at right angles and to be seventy-five to eighty feet wide.

Instantly, as though some medieval curse had been removed, San Francisco sprang to life. Within a few days news arrived from Washington that the cargoes of American vessels would be admitted duty-free into the harbor; word of this promptly spread through the maritime world. Then General Kearny released to San Francisco from United States Government ownership a large block of land consisting of the beach and water lots on the eastern front of the town facing the bay. On March 6 another decisive event took place: the first of four army transports dropped anchor in the bay and began discharging a thousand volunteers who had joined up on the condition that when their term of service was over they would be allowed to remain in California. Many of these men were skilled mechanics; they brought not only an incomparable source of manpower to the newly rebaptized city, but army tools, army supplies and army pay, all of them needed in the building of the town.

On March 16 Edwin Bryant, whose *What I Saw in California* was published the following year, and who had succeeded Bartlett as alcalde of San Francisco, offered up lots in the new tract for sale, particularly those on the waterfront and extending out into the bay so that wharves and jetties might be built to receive incoming ships, and warehouses to store the arriving merchandise.

In May the *Californian*, the newspaper started in Monterey by the Reverend Walter Colton and Robert Semple, transferred its press and operations to San Francisco. The arrival of the newspaper was a tacit admission that in a few short months San Francisco had become the most important settlement in central California. Monterey, which was struggling to maintain its position as the capital of California, received another severe blow, administered to a group of entrepreneurs who were trying to bring in fresh industry: fifty gamblers had moved into Monterey and opened a monte game. The cards had hardly gotten warm before Alcalde Colton surrounded their hotel with a troop of soldiers, arrested the gambling ring and sent them scattering. Most of them took their talents to the growing metropolis of San Francisco, where they would be appreciated.

By June of 1847 the population of San Francisco had risen to three hundred seventy-five whites; four fifths of the population was under forty years of age, making the city one of the world's youngest populations. From its inception San Francisco was international, with men from the United States, Mexico, Canada, England, France, Germany, Ireland, Scotland, Switzerland, Denmark, New Zealand, Peru, Poland, Russia, the Sandwich Islands, Sweden and the West Indies. Most of the professions and occupations were also represented: twenty-six carpenters, twenty laborers, thirteen clerks, eleven farmers and eleven merchants, seven bakers and seven butchers, six blacksmiths and six brickmakers, five grocers, four each of masons, shoemakers, tailors, three each of lawyers, doctors, coopers, hotel keepers; two tanners; two gunsmiths; a schoolteacher, brewer, cigar maker, gardener, miner, Morocco-case maker, navigator, painter, saddler and watchmaker. By now there were eight general stores, seven groceries, three butcher shops and bakeries, two hotels and two printing offices.

In September the first City Council was elected by popular ballot. Democratic government took over in San Francisco.

Once the army, with Kearny riding at its head and Fremont bringing up the rear, had departed from the Sacramento Valley a new wave of enterprise swept over Sutter's Fort as well. Sutter was building new granaries, a new threshing floor and outbuildings, sending exploring parties to find fresh sources of the lumber which he needed for "barrels, shingles, rafts and boats, for wagons, spinning-wheels and weaving-looms, for pumps to irrigate his vegetable gardens, for fences, for the making of charcoal needed in the smithy, and the bark of the oak for the tannery."

John Sutter was now forty-four years of age and at the height of his powers. Sometimes he sat at his desk until four o'clock in the morning writing letters and messages which his couriers carried on swift horses. He was delivering grain and cattle, hides, hats, a dozen other products produced in his shops. Still described by people visiting the fort as being in looks and manner "an old school gentleman," he was growing stout, his good-looking face a little florid, his clear blue eyes still twinkling, his manner totally charming. He had a well-tended mustache and side whiskers, never left his office without his silver-topped cane, the mace of authority in California: the Patriarch of the Sacramento Valley.

The war had hurt John Sutter by stopping many of the activities at the fort; the supplies and animals he had unstintingly provided John Fremont, taking government scrip in return, now seemed lost because Kearny had declared Fremont's scrip worthless. The possessions he had sent out to help rescue the Donners and other emigrant parties would almost surely be unreturned. He had not been able to supply enough wheat to wipe out any notable part of the $30,000 price he had paid the Russians for Fort Ross. Sutter calculated his debts to be somewhere between $80,000 and $100,000, all of it used to open and develop the country, to start new ranches and industries.

In late August 1847 he was in process of building a large flour mill five miles up the American River, a mill which he believed could pay off all of his debt, but he was held up for lack of lumber. What he needed was a sawmill high in the mountains, where there were magnificent stands of timber.

On August 25 there arrived at the fort the first contingent of the Mormon Battalion, which had been disbanded in southern California and was making its way back east to rejoin family and friends. The men settled two miles from the fort on the American River awaiting news from Brigham Young. Within a day or two Captain John Brown came into the Sacramento Valley from Great Salt Lake to buy cattle and feed for the Saints, and to bring instructions to the young Mormons: Brigham Young and the Elders urged them to remain where they were over the winter, to work and earn what money they could.

The Mormons were young, vigorous, good workers and many of them skilled mechanics, the one commodity for which Sutter had hungered from the day of his arrival. They now offered to go to work for Sutter. Because of this unexpected windfall, on August 27 Sutter entered into a contract with his carpenter, James Wilson Marshall, to build a sawmill on a spot recommended by Marshall, fifty miles up the south fork of the American River.

John Bidwell, Sutter's most devoted friend and adviser, was aghast at the foolhardiness of the project. He did everything he could to dissuade Sutter from pouring into the mountain wilderness the stream of wagons, provisions, tools and raw materials necessary to build a sawmill. But Sutter was visioning visions: the sawmill would bring him the finest lumber ever known in California; the Mormons would be able to complete construction of his flour mill. Bidwell said:

"It is hard to conceive how any sane man could have selected such a site for a sawmill. Surely no other man than Marshall ever entertained so wild a scheme as that of rafting sawed lumber down the canyons of the American River, and no other man than Sutter would have been so confiding and credulous as to patronize him."

As far as Sutter's future was concerned, Bidwell proved to be right, but for the wrong reasons. Since Sutter had on hand his fine supply of earnest laborers and mechanics, all of whom he would lose in the spring when they made their way over the mountains to Great Salt Lake, he decided that this was a God-given opportunity. He heartily joined Marshall's wild gamble.

Thus it was that in the year 1847 the Mormons not only settled Bonneville's Lake, bringing a whole new people and new culture to the Far West, but the presence of members of the Mormon Battalion, poising at Sutter's for the winter, was also instrumental in bringing to California, traversing Colorado, Utah and Nevada en route, the greatest rush of humanity ever to pour into a country from every radius of the earth's circumference.

CHAPTER XXVII

"It's GOLD!"

JAMES W. MARSHALL WAS A WESTERING WANDERER, a solitary, silent, sometimes cantankerous and almost totally friendless master carpenter who was born in Hunterdon County, New Jersey, on October 8, 1810, given some moderate book education, but mostly trained by his father who was a coach and wagon builder. He had earned his living as an itinerant carpenter first in Crawfordsville, Indiana, then in Warsaw, Illinois, then continued his wandering until he located a homestead near Fort Leavenworth, on the frontier, built a fairly prosperous farm, and might have been content to remain there had he not suffered from the Missouri fever and ague.

At the end of six years he gave up the struggle and, having heard of California, joined a caravan of a hundred wagons leaving Missouri on May 1, 1844. Marshall had no wagon, he was on horseback, traveling alone and carrying his kit of carpenter's tools. He wintered in Oregon, then came south to California in June of 1845 with the Clyman-McMahon Party. By July he was at Sutter's Fort and most gratefully employed by Sutter as a mechanic, building spinning wheels for blanket weavers, mending the fort wagons, putting up outbuildings. Within a period of a year Marshall had accumulated enough money to buy a ranch. He also put in a small herd of cattle, and appeared content to settle down as a rancher when he became involved with the California Battalion and spent a number of months as a soldier.

When Marshall returned at the end of the war, *sans* pay, he found that his cattle had either been stolen or wandered off. Having no funds with which to begin again, he sold his land and went back to work for Sutter. But in the spring of 1847 Marshall, not yet thirty-seven, ambitious, and unwilling to work out the rest of his life as an employed carpenter, went to his boss and proposed that Sutter lend him an Indian guide so that he could explore the mountain river country, find a good spot for a sawmill in the midst of the lumber supply of the Sierra Nevada, and float the lumber down the river to Sutter's Fort. At first Sutter thought this a harebrained idea; however Marshall had his heart set on the sawmill project. Why he chose the particular spot of Culloomah, as Coloma was known by the Indians, is best told in Marshall's own words:

"The river here flowed through the centre of a narrow valley, hemmed in on both sides by steep, and in some parts almost precipitous hills...the river makes several bends in its course through this valley, and on the south side a point of land formed by one of these curves in the stream presented the explorer with the mill site he was in search of. The water power was abundant, and the surrounding hills furnished timber in apparently inexhaustible quantities."

James Marshall was a taciturn, phlegmatic man with considerable driving power. His securing of a contract, money, supplies and men from Sutter was the first step in his determination to become a man of substance.

With the turn of the New Year, 1848, the mill was completed, but there was a structural defect which Marshall had to correct: the tailrace was too shallow at its end, so that the dammed-up water rushed back and prevented the flutter wheel from turning. The channel had to be deepened by blasting.

On the morning of January 24 Marshall closed the gate which shut off the water from the river, then walked down the forebay or tailrace, to see whether the flow of water had removed the sand and gravel during the night. What happened was set down later by Marshall's biographer:

"Having strolled to the lower end of the race, he stood for a moment examining the mass of debris that had been washed down, and his eye caught the glitter of something that lay, lodged in a crevice, on a riffle of soft granite, some six inches under the water. He picked up the substance. It was heavy, of a peculiar color, and unlike anything he had seen in the stream before. For a few minutes he stood with it in his hand, endeavoring to recall all that he had heard or read concerning the various minerals. The weight assured him that it could not be mica. Could it be sulphurets of copper? He remembered that that mineral is brittle; he turned about, placed the specimen under a flat stone and proceeded to test it by striking it with another. The substance did not crack or flake off; it simply bent under the blow."

Marshall returned to the mill, his usually crusty face beaming, and cried: "Boys, by God, I believe I have found a gold mine!"

He showed his nuggets as proof. His workers were not impressed. They continued about their tasks. On the morning of the fifth day, after having in the course of his inspection of the tailrace and of the shallow side of the river selected several more yellow nuggets, enough to make three ounces tied in his kerchief, Marshall started out on horseback to cover the fifty mountain miles down to the fort, sleeping that night under an oak tree. He was ostensibly searching for a wagonload of supplies which Sutter had promised.

At nine o'clock on the morning of January 28, 1848, sopping wet from a cloudburst which had enveloped him in the last eight miles, Marshall arrived at the fort. He asked Sutter where they could talk with privacy. Puzzled, Sutter took him to his bedroom, sitting room in the main building, locking the door. Marshall asked for two bowls of water, a stick of redwood and some twine and

sheet copper to make a scales. Sutter told him that he had scales in the apoth-
ecary shop and went for them himself, failing to lock the bedroom door when
he returned. A clerk walked in with some papers just as Marshall was about to
dump the yellow nuggets onto the table. Marshall cried in consternation:

"There! Didn't I tell you we had listeners!"

Sutter quieted his overwrought partner, then gazed down at the yellow
nuggets which James Marshall poured out of his kerchief onto the table. Sutter
examined the specimens, pulled down a volume of his *Encyclopedia Americana*,
studied it for a time, tested the nuggets with *aquafortis*, which had no effect on
them, balanced them on the scales with a like amount of silver, then dipped the
scales into water, the yellow nuggets quickly outweighing the silver.

Sutter turned his now wide and flashing eyes up into the face of the wildly
excited Marshall.

"It's gold," Sutter said. "At least twenty-three-carat gold!"

CHAPTER XXVIII

"A frenzy seized my soul"

THE FORTY-EIGHTER, in pursuit of gold, was a reluctant bride groom. His portrait bears little relation to his highly publicized cousin, the Forty-Niner, yet in many ways he is the more interesting, or at least purer, personality. Sutter, Marsh, Vallejo, Larkin, Bidwell, Hartnell, Robinson made their hesitant way into the hills, but they did not stay long, and few took out any appreciable sum. The early settlers had not come to California for gold, yet how could a man justify his not stooping to pick up the essence of wealth when all he had to do was scratch it out with his pocket knife?

John Sutter and James Marshall tried to keep their discovery secret, Sutter extracting a promise from the workmen at Coloma to remain for the six weeks necessary to get the sawmill into operation. He also urged his employees at the mill to say nothing of the nuggets. But for a surprising length of time there was no secret to leak: the workmen thought these few gold nuggets to be in the American River by chance. They continued with their tasks. All, that is, except young Henry Bigler, one of the Mormon Battalion working for Sutter; on Sunday young Bigler picked up his gun as though he were going hunting, crossed the stream out of sight of his comrades and searched for gold. He found a few particles. The next day after work he scratched up a little more. The following Sunday he found a full ounce, and on Washington's Birthday he went out in a snowstorm, still ostensibly to hunt game, unearthing a nugget. When he returned to the mill, wet and frozen, his companions demanded an explanation. Bigler untied his shirt tail, scattering $22.50 worth of gold onto their crude table. He also confessed that he had written of his findings to their fellow Mormons at Sutter's flour mill.

Bigler did considerably better than his employer in keeping the secret, for on February 10, only thirteen days after Marshall's arrival at the fort with the packet of gold, the ebullient Sutter wrote to Vallejo:

"I have made a discovery of a gold mine which, according to experiments we have made, is extraordinarily rich."

Mariano Vallejo kept the secret without being asked to; like most Californios he knew from the outset that gold was the ultimate gamble.

Sutter, as had the Russians at Fort Ross before him, bought a three-year lease from the Indians around Coloma, the only two such instances on the record books of the Far West. If Sutter gave false reasons for acquiring his lease, it was not because he hoped to keep all the gold for himself, but rather because he needed a few more weeks to complete the work on his flour and sawmills.

By now the dozen employees at Sutter's sawmill, earning about a dollar a day and their keep, saw from Bigler's find that they could mine the American River with their pocket knives for ten to twenty times their wage. Yet not one man ran out on his promise to Sutter to work the six weeks necessary to complete the mill; they simply used their spare hours to go fishing for gold.

Henry Bigler, when he wrote to his Mormon companions at the flour mill, urged them to keep the matter secret but to come up for a short visit. Levi Fifield, Wilford Hudson and Sidney Willis accepted the invitation, came to Coloma and worked over the tailrace where Marshall had seen the first golden glints. Picking through the accumulated sand and gravel they found nuggets weighing in at $6.00. These three members of the Mormon Battalion, by traveling forty-six miles to look for gold, became the first Forty-Eighters.

On their return journey they stopped long enough to prospect on a sand bar about halfway down to Sutter's; here they found gold lying very close to the sand surface. By their stop of perhaps an hour they became the discoverers of Mormon Island, from which a fortune was subsequently taken by other prospectors.

Two things now happened simultaneously to break the news: one of Sutter's haulers, Jacob Wittmer, arriving at Coloma with a wagonful of materials and provisions, was told by one of the young Weimar boys:

"We have found gold up here."

When Wittmer ridiculed the idea, Mrs. Weimar gave the teamster a good-sized nugget as a gift to prove her son spoke the truth.

At the same moment John Sutter sent a Mormon in his employ, Charles Bennett, to the governor of California, Colonel R.B. Mason at Monterey, to secure a confirmation of his Indian lease. Bennett was ordered to say nothing about the discovery of gold, but when he met a group of prospectors searching for a coal mine near Dr. Marsh's rancho on Mount Diablo, this was too rare a joke to keep to himself: men grubbing for coal when there was gold lying all along the American River!

Bennett took out his pouch of gold dust and nuggets to convince the unbelieving coal prospectors.

Jacob Wittmer, arriving back at Sutter's fort, went into a general supply store that had been opened in one of Sutter's outbuildings by Samuel Brannan, ordered a bottle of brandy and put down Mrs. Weimar's gift on the counter to pay for it. Brannan's partner, George Smith, sent for Brannan; they refused to believe this nugget was gold, even as the coal-mining prospectors had refused to believe Bennett's evidence. Jacob Wittmer had no recourse but to send for Captain John Sutter.

Sutter could not lie with the nugget staring back at him from the counter. He confirmed the discovery. The date was February 15, 1848. On the same day Charles Bennett reached San Francisco and showed the gold dust to everyone who would look. With the exception of one man, Isaac Humphrey, a former gold miner from Georgia, nobody believed it was gold. Isaac Humphrey bought a pick, shovel, basin and materials to build a rocker, and left all alone for the hundred-fifty-mile journey to Coloma, the first man of the Exodus.

There was no valid reason for San Francisco to grow excited about a rumor of gold in the distant Sierra Nevada; since that day in 1846 when Fremont had spiked the rusty guns of the presidio the forsaken hamlet of half a dozen mud huts on the cove had grown to a community of two hundred buildings. Two fair-sized hotels had been built, two wharves, warehouses, twelve stores, some of them representing long-established firms in the East and Honolulu. There were billiard and tenpin alleys, an advertisement in the *Star* on March 1, 1848 for a schoolteacher, and on March 5 a public sale of town lots found fifty-two buyers at an average and gratifying price of $22.50. San Francisco might soon become the great city of the Pacific coast, center of trade from the East and Europe and the Orient. The *Californian* reported the discovery of gold on March 15, and the *Star* on the eighteenth, but in a quiet, back-page line.

Now, almost two months after the discovery, Marshall's sawmill was completed; about the twentieth of March the first logs were sawed into planks. Having proved that the sawmill they built could work, the entire crew quit and went prospecting. As John Caughey says in *Gold Is the Cornerstone*:

"The instrument of discovery thus fell victim to the overpowering force that it unloosed."

John Sutter suddenly had the roof over his empire fall in on him: the staff of his just completed $30,000 flour mill also resigned and struck out for the mountains. The tanners in their shop at the fort caught the fever and walked out on two thousand fresh hides which rotted away. His long-time crew of Indians showed admirable restraint in remaining long enough to harvest the forty-thousand-bushel wheat crop, then vanished silently in the night, leaving Sutter's wheat to spoil in the sun because there was no one to thresh, any more than there was anyone to complete the shoes, hats, barrels, blankets or any of the dozen other articles that Sutter had been manufacturing.

Thus Sutter, who had caused the gold to be discovered, also provided the manpower for the official start of the gold rush.

It was Sam Brannan who acted as the catalyst for the outside world. Having milked Mormonism of its last procurable tithe from the Battalion boys in the gold fields, Sam now abandoned the Latter-day Saints, who returned the compliment by excommunicating him for a second time. Clever opportunist, high-powered adventurer, shrewd trader and manipulator, Brannan burst into San Francisco on May 12, riding horseback through the streets, waving his hat over his head and crying at the top of his lungs:

"Gold! Gold! Gold from the American River!"

His histrionics galvanized a city which two months before had gazed indifferently at Bennett's pouch.

Sailors in the harbor deserted their ships, their captains right behind them. Doctors walked out on their patients, judges on their supplicants, the mayor and his city council on their citizens . . . most of whom were already gone. The little school, after its brave start, had to close, the two newspapers shut down for lack of printers, as did the stores because there were neither clerks to sell nor customers to buy. Soldiers walked off their posts and never returned; hotels had neither managers nor guests; farmers made for the hills, leaving their grains and vegetables to die. Property which had been valuable a few days before was hawked for half price with no takers. Within a matter of days the city looked as though a plague had struck it, with only one fourth of its male population left.

In Monterey, when the first gold was shown on the streets, the town emptied out so completely that the Reverend Walter Colton ruefully reported: "A general of the United States Army, the commander of a man-of-war and the Alcalde of Monterey, in a smoking kitchen, grinding coffee, toasting a herring and peeling onions!"

Commodore Thomas Ap Catesby Jones, who had inadvertently seized Monterey in 1842, now found that as commander of the Pacific Squadron he did not have enough sailors left to capture Catalina Island.

Sailors who, by jumping ship to get to the mines, sacrificed four years pay, must have felt the way another goldrusher did when he gazed upon the well-filled pouch of a digger:

"A frenzy seized my soul; houses were too small for me to stay in; I was soon in the street in search of necessary outfits; piles of gold rose up before me at every step; castles of marble, dazzling the eye with their rich appliances; thousands of slaves bowing to my beck and call; myriads of fair virgins contending with each other for my love...were among the fancies of my favored imagination. The Rothschilds and Astors appeared to me but poor people; in short I had a very violent attack of the gold fever."

As actual bags of gold began to come down from the mountains, town after town emptied out in dramatic fashion. Sonoma, which had just been laid out as a city and subdivided into lots, "lost two-thirds of its inhabitants. Most of its houses are empty, all work has stopped and here, as every where else, there is not a single carpenter left nor a joiner nor a blacksmith nor any laborer to do the least work."

Thomas O. Larkin wrote from San Jose that "everyone had gold or yellow fever. Nine-tenths of every storekeeper, mechanic and day laborer leave for the Sacramento."

Luis Peralta, an aging Californio gentleman who had been given a vast grant comprising the present cities of Berkeley, Oakland and Alameda, refused to be stampeded. He said:

"My sons, God has given this gold to the Americans. Had he desired us to have it, He would have given it to us ere now. Therefore, go not after it, but let others go. Plant your lands, and reap; these be your best gold fields, for all must eat while they live."

Mariano Vallejo rode up to Coloma, watched other men successfully mining gold, picked up a few flakes as a matter of scientific interest, then rode back to his home in Sonoma, never again bothering to go into the gold fields. Nor did the Californio families from San Luis Obispo south join the rush; they remained on their land and within a year, as Luis Peralta had predicted to his sons, found that their herds of cattle were richer gold fields than Coloma or Mormon Island.

CHAPTER XXIX

It's as Easy to Find Gold as Steal It

THE GOLD THAT HAD BEEN FREED from its deposit in the mountains had been carried by the rivers of the Sierra Nevada. The streams naturally found their way down canyons and declivities; the sun circled over the cool, heavily timbered areas for perhaps a couple of hours a day, hardly enough to warm or dry the ravines.

The prospectors were getting their feet wet in some of the coldest melted-snow water to tumble down a mountainside.

Aside from Marshall's settlement in the fairly wide valley at Coloma there were no towns, no houses, no food and no roads on which to get in. The first prospectors from Sutter's went into the mountains on horseback or on foot, carrying a blanket roll inside of which they cached such provisions as were available: flour, bacon, coffee. Dangling from the straps of the blanket roll was the triumvirate of the tenderfoot: a pick, a shovel and a frying pan, all a man allegedly needed to found his fortune.

Reaching the mines from San Francisco was an involved process; prospectors either had to cross the wide bay or make the forty-mile journey down the peninsula almost to San Jose, and then double back northward. Rowboats that had been worth $50 now sold at $500. Wagon trains drawn by oxen or mules made the circling land movement around the bay but the largest number of the prospectors went on foot, rifle in hand. One man crossed alone on Robert Semple's ferry at Martinez late in April 1848; two weeks later he found a hundred wagons waiting for the ferry with a small army of men inside a wide ring of campfires, each name written on a waiting list.

John Bidwell, who had been told immediately by Sutter of Marshall's discovery, made a careful examination of the terrain around Coloma and decided that it was similar to the country on the Feather River where he had bought a large ranch. He returned north, found light particles of gold far down the Feather River and reasoned that the heavier particles would remain near the hills. At Chico he organized his friends and neighbors. Bidwell says that in nearly all the places they prospected they found the color, but his companions felt the gold they were panning was too light, and lit out for the American River.

Bidwell and two friends continued up the Feather River, soon striking a rich deposit which became known as Bidwell's Bar. By discovering the color thirty miles to the north of Coloma, Bidwell opened the entire area as possible gold country.

Pierson B. Reading, who had come in with the Chiles group in 1843 and was ranching at the extreme north of the central California valley, followed Bidwell's example, studied the terrain at Coloma and returned home to find gold on Clear Creek near his own land. Men now fanned out in all directions looking for geographical situations similar to Coloma. By May prospectors were taking out the metal some ten miles west of Coloma toward Sutter's, and ten miles east, deep into the heart of the Sierra Nevada.

Men on foot, searching for new and promising diggings on all the forks and tributaries, laid their blanket rolls under the trees, then built campfires. Those who had come on horseback or with wagons sometimes had tents; a few of the more experienced had brought axes with which to cut timber and build a lean-to. Some anchored their wagons with rocks and slept in them. Thus were the first mining towns born. Few of those who came in on foot could remain more than a week; that was as long as their provisions lasted. There was no way to buy a morsel of food. Most of the prospectors had been skeptical, but what they found or saw others finding sent them back to Sutter's and sometimes all the way back to San Francisco to settle their affairs, buy all the food and tools their money would provide and strike out again, this time to stay.

By July some two thousand Americans were in the mining regions, with another two thousand Californios and Indians working alongside them. With the passing of the months four thousand more Americans, including deserting sailors and soldiers, came to prospect, crawling over the foothills of the Sierra Nevada picking up all the gold in sight.

The first miners to reach the diggings did not bother to stake out claims. They skimmed over the waterways scooping up the surface gold, quickly moving on. As their number increased and knowledge spread as to the gold-bearing potential of each camp or gulch, the men came together at the new general store and held a meeting to decide the size of the claim that each man could call his own, varying from ten feet square in the early camps to ten feet from the center of the stream all the way back to the base of the hills. The setting down of a man's pick or shovel on the spot was enough to make his claim legal.

These first informal meetings were the beginnings of self- government in the mountain mines; Colonel Mason was the military governor of the state, stationed in Monterey, but no other government existed. As Charles H. Shinn says in *Mining Camps*:

"The miners needed no criminal code. It is simply and literally true that there was a short time in California, in 1848, when crime was almost absolutely unknown, when pounds and pints of gold were left unguarded in tents and cabins, or thrown down on the hillside, or handed about through a crowd for inspection. An old pioneer writes me that, 'In 1848 a man could go into a miner's cabin, cut a slice of bacon, cook a meal, roll up in a blanket, and go to sleep, certain to be welcomed kindly when the owner returned.' Men have told me that they have known as much as a washbasinful of gold-dust to be left on the table in an open tent while the owners were at work in their claim a mile distant."

It was as easy to find gold as steal it. Anybody taking his neighbor's gold would be stealing more for fun than profit. One or two tried it toward the end of the year and were hanged without trial or tears.

The mountains were arcadia during 1848; the miners were young, there were no social distinctions, and if one man found a considerable lay of gold today, tomorrow would be his neighbor's turn. Friends or neighbors made a common pot of their food, each man cooking in turn. The result was frequently poor but "no man shall grumble at the cook's failures, under penalty of cooking for twice the usual period." Everyone was open-handed to new arrivals. Shinn reports the story of a ten-year-old boy who arrived in camp alone, starved and without the essential tools for even the simplest mining. The men at the diggings agreed to work one hour for the boy, at the end of that time turning over to him enough gold dust to buy a complete outfit, and the stricture that he would now have to "paddle for himself."

There was no social life in 1848. Few camps had even one woman, though later in the year a few arrived with their husbands to open restaurants or boardinghouses. At night, after work, the men gathered around campfires, spinning yarns, speaking nostalgically of home or their journey to California while they sat in the blackness surrounded by strange giant trees and mountains. Friendship was their greatest pleasure; in this all-male society partnerships were formed that have been described by participants as "indissoluble as marriage." The only family life was that of the Californios, who brought their wives, children and Indian servants, the families dancing in the evenings "on the green, before the tents." The young Americans found it "quite a treat, after a hard day's work, to go at nightfall to one of these fandangoes."

This sylvan aspect lasted almost to the end of 1848, though by late fall the outside influx had begun: Californios up from southern California; the first out-of-state goldrushers from Oregon; four thousand native Mexicans from Sonora; the first gold-rush arrivals by sea, an early contingent from Hawaii and another from Chile.

By October winter descended upon the mountains, with rain, snow and intense cold. A few of the more hardy decided to remain and built rude log cabins. Eight hundred men stayed on at Dry Diggings, later called Hangtown, then Placerville, taking out about five ounces a day. The vast majority, with the waters in the river unendurably icy, made their way out of the hills and into the warmer plains. Some had made their pile, many were disappointed and sick, ragged, grim and bespotted:

"Cursing the country and their hard fate."

By the beginning of September San Francisco had ceased to be a ghost town. Men had begun to return from the mines, some feverish to spend their pouches of gold, others just feverish. By October enough of the City Council had returned to hold a meeting, and one hundred fifty-eight returnees cast their ballots in the alcalde election. At this encouraging sign real estate went up fifty per cent, one courageous soul erecting the first brick house ever built in San Francisco; stores and merchandise that had been hawked for any price they would bring went back to their pre-gold values, and by December land and buildings were selling for double what they had cost.

Enough printers as well as subscribers had returned from the mines for the earliest California papers, the *Star* and the *Californian* to combine and resume publishing; and by December 12 the public school, which had opened for a few weeks in the spring, resumed classes with tuition set at $8.00 a term, probably the best buy in a city where it now took $100 in gold dust to buy a blanket, a pair of boots or a gallon of whiskey.

San Francisco appointed the Reverend T.D. Hunt, a Presbyterian, as town chaplain and the Reverend Mr. Hunt officiated at the first Protestant services, aside from the Mormons', to be held in San Francisco. In San Jose there was a first meeting of Americans looking toward the formation of a government for California, which now had only an alcalde and council in San Francisco, the Reverend Mr. Colton as alcalde in Monterey, acaldes in Santa Barbara and Los Angeles. Colonel Mason, military governor of the "possession," had so little power that his plan to establish license fees where gold was being dug, in order to collect taxes with which to run the country, was never attempted, most of his army having deserted. However he did assure the people that the United States Congress would soon:

"Confer on them the constitutional rights of citizens of the United States."

Emigration across the plains from Missouri in the spring months of 1848 had been modest. Captain Chiles, who had led a small horseback party through Nevada in 1843, had brought in forty-eight wagons with perhaps one hundred fifty people. Bancroft's *Register* shows only five hundred twenty names of incoming pioneers.

But few phenomena inflame the mind of man so universally as the discovery of gold. For word had to get out: ships leaving San Francisco Harbor plowing the seas to Honolulu, Victoria, Vancouver; members of the Mormon Battalion traveling to Salt Lake; a letter from L.W. Boggs to his brother in Oregon, other letters written by young men wanting to tell their families and friends all over the country about their adventures.

The Baltimore *Sun* had run the first newspaper story about the gold discovery in September, quickly followed by articles in the New York *Herald* and the New York *Journal of Commerce*. But they were too exaggerated to be believed:

"People are running over the country and picking it out of the earth here and there just as 1,000 hogs let loose in a forest would root up ground nuts."

The official reports were more important: Thomas Larkin's report to Secretary of State Buchanan sent east by the flagship *Ohio*; Colonel Mason's report to the Adjutant General, accompanied by either a tea caddy or an oyster can full of gold for visual and tactile proof, sent to Buchanan.

President Polk incorporated Colonel Mason's report in his message to Congress on December 9, 1848, publicly displaying the gold at the War Office, and crying:

"The accounts of the abundance of gold are of such an extraordinary character, as would scarcely command belief were they not corroborated by the authentic reports of officers in the public service."

That would do it.

CHAPTER XXX

What Gambler Ever Refused to Play?

HOW MUCH DID THE FORTY-EIGHTERS take out of the river-beds, sand bars and loose rock? It varied according to a man's strength, ambition and luck. At first nearly everyone could pan from $10 to $15 of gold dust if he worked from dawn to dark. Considering the fact that in San Francisco prior to the discovery a cook received $25 to $30 a month and a clerk $50 to $60, these were considered good findings.

As in all such strikes there were the fortunate ones: John Sullivan, an Irish teamster who had been earning $5.00 a day, took out $26,000 from the diggings named after him on the Stanislaus River. A man named Hudson obtained some $20,000 in six weeks from a canyon between Coloma and the American middle fork. A boy called Davenport found seventy-seven ounces of pure gold one day and ninety ounces the next. At Dry Diggings a Mr. Wilson took $2000 from under his doorstep. Three Frenchmen discovered gold in removing a stump which obstructed the road from Dry Diggings to Coloma and within a week dug up $5000. On the Yuba River middle fork one man picked up nearly thirty pounds of gold from a piece of ground less than four feet square. Amador relates that he saw diggings which yielded $8.00 to every spadeful of earth. He and a companion, with twenty native laborers, took out from seven to nine pounds of gold a day. Robert Birnie, an employee of British Consul Forbes, saw miners at Dry Diggings mining from fifty to a hundred ounces daily.

Soule, who was the closest of the California historians to the gold rush, tells in his *Annals of San Francisco*:

"Well authenticated accounts described many known persons as averaging from one to two hundred a day for a long period. Numerous others were said to be earning from five to eight hundred dollars a day. If, indeed, a man with a pick and pan did not easily gather some thirty or forty dollars worth of dust in a single day, he just moved off to some other place which he supposed might be richer."

A correspondent of the *Californian* wrote from Dry Diggings in the middle of August 1848 that "the earth is taken out of the ravines and is carried in wagons and packed on horses from one to three miles to the water, where it is washed; $400 has been an average for a cart load. Instances have occurred here where men have carried the earth on their backs, and collected from $800 to

$1500 in a day." But there were complications in the golden paradise. Men unaccustomed to hard physical labor found that working knee- deep in the icy water all day, filling a pan or an Indian basket with dirt, lowering it into the water, then shaking the pan vigorously to wash out the sand and clay; sleeping at night in the cold and dampness; eating little more than bacon, sourdough bread and coffee brought them down with colds, fevers, pneumonia, dysentery. With their rudimentary equipment they could mine but shallowly, and the surface gold was quickly exhausted. Though they might earn well for a few weeks they would then have to go scurrying over the mountains looking for fresh deposits.

The supplies which now began to come in over the Indian trails took their prices not merely from the costs of hauling: freighters charged $300 to transport three barrels of flour, one of pork and two hundred pounds of small stores the fifty miles from Sutter's to the diggings; but also from the belief that the men who pick up wealth from the ground should share it with those self-sacrificing enough to deny themselves this great opportunity. Pans worth twenty cents now cost from $8.00 to $16. A fifty-cent box of Seidlitz powders cost $24. Every pill, regardless of its value, cost $1.00. Forty drops of laudanum cost $40. Shirts sold at $16 apiece. The Reverend Mr. Colton, touring the mining area in October, wrote: "We pay at the rate of $400 a barrel for flour; $4.00 a pound for poor brown sugar, and $4.00 a pound for indifferent coffee. And as for meat, there is none to be got except jerked-beef, which is the flesh of the bullock cut into strings and hung up in the sun to dry." As entrepreneurs came into the camps to build little hotels and restaurants, prices went even higher. A breakfast at Coloma consisting of a box of sardines, bread, butter, cheese and two bottles of ale cost $43.

By the fall of 1848 those prospectors who were mining an ounce a day, about half of the mining population, were spending their ounce for the basic necessities and consequently were working for their keep. Another quarter, dogged by bad luck or just slower, found that they could not average the ounce a day necessary to live on, and had to go to work for someone who could guarantee their food. The remaining quarter took out a profit ranging from a few hundred dollars to sizable fortunes, the latter accumulated by perhaps five per cent of the prospectors.

What gambler ever refused to play because the odds were heavily against him? No attention was paid to the exhausted, the sick and emaciated who returned, though some of them lay ill for months and many died. The ones who caused the great excitement were those who returned to the towns flashing a pouch full of gold; then another wave of humanity started for the mines.

Even Thomas O. Larkin, who had said, "We cannot imagine the bad results to California if this fever continues," finally could not resist forming a company with the foreman of his Sacramento Valley rancho and a clerk in his office at Monterey to round up all the Indians they could find and go into the mines on shares. He also sent in a supply of goods with which to open a general store.

Dr. John Marsh organized a company among his neighbors. They loaded pack animals with food and mining equipment, donned the red shirts and boots which were becoming standard equipment for prospectors, and made their way north to the Yuba River. Here Dr. Marsh struck a rich bar, taking out $50 of gold an hour from the very beginning.

Larkin was satisfied with a modest three hundred per cent profit on his goods, but Marsh sold beads and sugar to the Indians at the rate of a cup of beads for a cup of gold! When he ran out of supplies he ended by selling the red shirt off his back to an enchanted Indian for $300. But Marsh, now forty-nine, was too old for this rugged existence. He became ill and had to return home, carrying with him $40,000 in gold for something under six months of work; a bonanza, if you don't mind getting sick, and selling the shirt off your back. Nor did John Bidwell stay with mining after his Indians went off to seek gold for themselves; he too opened a store.

Until his discovery of gold James W. Marshall had had little luck or success, partly because he was an irascible wanderer. His tenacity in finding a logical site for a sawmill and getting Sutter to stake him to it should have established him, but no one would work his mill. Throngs of incoming miners squatted on his land surrounding the mill and he could not get them off. His oxen, worth $400 per yoke, "went down into the canyon and thence down hungry men's throats." When he went prospecting he returned to find that migratory miners had taken his mill apart to use for their own purposes. Nor did he have any greater success as a miner; Sutter twice provided him with a prospector's outfit, but the spirits he believed were directing his search were apparently out prospecting on their own:

"Should I get to new localities and commence to open a new mine, numbers flocked in and commenced seeking all around me, and, as numbers tell, someone would find the lead before me, and the ground was claimed. Then I would travel again."

John Sutter, who had no help to run his sawmill, flour mill, tannery, or to thresh his grain, compensated for his losses by opening a store at the fort, which was on the main line to the mines, renting out space to merchants. He also grubstaked several prospectors on a share-and-share basis. He declared optimistically:

"There is no need for me to go into the mountains to make my pile of gold, the gold will flow to me."

The arrival of his twenty-two-year-old son August seemed a more discouraging prospect. It was the imminence of this son in Burgdorf which had obliged Sutter to marry August's mother and endure years of marital unhappiness. Sutter had never intended to see any member of his Swiss family again. When he heard that August was in San Francisco, John Sutter fled to Coloma where he prospected in the bottle, keeping himself drunk to wipe out the gnawing question of, Once the son had arrived, could the mother be far behind?

August Sutter proved to be a loyal and level-headed young man who might have saved his father from the utter ruin that now began to engulf him. August comments: "Indians, Negroes, Kanakas, and white men of any nation indiscriminately by applying to my father, easily obtained letters of credit from him to any amount for any stores then existing in or about the fort.... From the books I received I never could obtain any knowledge of the state of affairs on account of their dreadful confusion."

The widespread rumor that Sutter had been made a millionaire by the discovery of gold brought the rest of his past down upon him. Colonel Steward, new Russian consul in San Francisco arrived at the fort to collect about $31,000 still owed for Fort Ross. James Douglas, head of the Hudson's Bay Company, paid a personal visit to the fort to collect $7000 he claimed Sutter owed them. Antonio Suñol, a Californio neighbor, came to present a bill for $3000 for cattle and supplies. As the unkindest cut of all there arrived a Mr. French who claimed that Sutter owed him $3000 for the loan of the ship on which Sutter had sailed his cargo from Honolulu to Yerba Buena in 1839. Dozens of other creditors presented themselves. Captain John Sutter, who had given away a large part of his patrimony to exhausted emigrants, had only the vaguest notion of what he owed whom.

Half mad with the pressure and confusion, Sutter made his son the legal owner of his holdings and once again fled to the mountains. August faithfully set about the Herculean task of putting his father's accounts in order; the only way he found to do so was to agree to Sam Brannan's proposal that they create a town, to be called Sacramento City, between Sutter's Fort and the Embarcadero on the river, all of which land Sutter owned.

John Sutter had already laid out a town in 1846 which he had proudly named Sutterville. It was three miles down the river and safe from the yearly floods. A few buildings had been put up but the town was off the route to the gold mines and hence got no trade. Sacramento City was a hit from the moment August put the land on the market, enough cash coming in for him to pay off Douglas, Suñol, French and to give Consul Steward $10,000 in cash and $21,000 in lot values in Sacramento. Steward then absconded with the money, the Russians never getting a penny out of Fort Ross. .

In a matter of months Sacramento City, a tent and lean-to town, sprang into existence. Sutter's Fort found itself out in the country, abandoned. August sold it for $40,000.

All this money could have paid Sutter's debts many times over, except that Sutter was gone, wandering aimlessly, and the overconscientious son paid all claims presented to him, whether fabricated or real.

Sam Brannan next hatched a conspiracy to cheat the Sutters out of the best of the remaining land of Sacramento City, succeeding so brilliantly that August went down with a fever...though not before arranging to have his mother, two sisters and brother brought from Switzerland. In his illness August returned to his father the legal ownership of his estate; but what had been a vast property only two years before was now gone. Nothing remained but the Hock Farm, the first one that Sutter had cultivated outside his fort.

Here Sutter moved with his personal possessions. Onto the Hock Farm came the family from whom he had fled fourteen years before. Here Sutter lived without money, his family doing the house and farm work, but remaining the patriarchal figure of California, visited by hordes of people all of whom he tried to feed and entertain in the grand manner, even as he had at Sutter's Fort.

The discovery of gold had undone him.

By the end of 1848 there were some eight to ten thousand miners in the Sierra Nevada. By the end of the year $10,000,000 worth of gold had been dug out of the golden rectangle, of which $2,000,000 was shipped east to establish credit; $2,000,000 was consumed by the miners in food, clothing and utensils, animals, medications and drink; another $1,000,000 was spent in building the hundred-odd mining communities, a few of which became permanent towns, the majority vanishing when the gold was exhausted. Of the remaining $5,000,000 about half would have been taken by successful miners to their home towns: Sonoma, San Francisco, San Jose, Santa Cruz, Monterey, to be invested in ranches, business and residential property, and to buy or build stores, shops, hotels, homes.

Some of the balance would be saved by thrifty individuals like Dr. John Marsh, but most of it would be spent on luxuries by the comfort-starved miners returning after months of isolation in the mountains, or transferred from excitement-hungry miners to the black pockets of the early gamblers.

The $10,000,000 taken out in gold represented two thirds of the price paid by the United States to Mexico for the Far West, Texas, parts of New Mexico, Arizona and Wyoming, an area of over half a million square miles, between fifteen and twenty per cent of the contemporary United States.

Chapter XXXI

The Men Do Not Match the Mountains

JOHN FREMONT'S FOURTH EXPEDITION into the Far West was superbly organized. Carrying with him $10,000 worth of equipment and scientific instruments, a portion of which represented his own savings, it included Charles Preuss, the topographer who had been with Fremont since his First Expedition; Antoine Morin and Vincent Tabeau, French voyageurs who had been on the Second Expedition; Charles Taplin, a frontiersman; Thomas E. Breckenridge, an experienced westerner; John Scott, a hunter; a man named Long; and three California Indians. There were twelve greenhorns along but most of them were scientists, like Frederick Creutzfeldt, a botanist, whose stamina was equal to their dedication.

Fremont reached Bent's Fort in the midst of one of the earliest and severest winters Colorado had known; or so he was told by the Indians. His friend Kit Carson, who had given up his ranch and left his wife for the Third Expedition, could not see his way clear to leaving his family and farm again. Broken Hand Fitzpatrick maintained that as a federal Indian agent he could not leave his post. For a guide Fremont was obliged to settle on Old Bill Williams, wintering in Pueblo to nurse a bullet-shattered arm which he had received fighting against the Utes. Past sixty now, cantankerous Old Bill was an expert mountain man who knew the southern Rockies. To Fremont's question of whether he could get the party through, Old Bill replied:

"Sure, but there'll be trouble."

Now, at Hardscrabble, Fremont's party enjoyed the warmth of adobe cabins for a couple of days while they shucked the corn to be loaded into the packs of their train of more than a hundred first-rate mules. There would be enough food to enable the mules to survive for twenty-five days from Hardscrabble over the three ranges of mountains: the Wet, the Sangre de Cristo and the San Juans, the central bastions of the Rockies, and down into what later came to be known as Gunnison Valley, where there would be grass.

Old Bill Williams rode in the lead, "his body bent over his saddlehorn, across which rested a long heavy rifle, his keen grey eyes peering from under the slouched brim of a flexible felt hat, black and shining with grease."

The Wet Mountains had been accurately named: snows clogged the canyons, which were also choked by thick stands of aspen. The mules fell against the trees and rocks, ripping off their packs and losing corn. At nine thousand feet there was no water. In the Wet Mountain Valley there was no game. Though the journey was in its first days Dr. Ben Kern wrote in his diary, "After wading through the slush of melting snow . . . all very tired."

Old Bill decreed that they take the Robidoux Pass over the Sangre de Cristo Mountains. They struck heavy snows and a screaming gale. Campfires were impossible to sustain. "The winds were caught in the valley and never got out, and then blew wildly in all directions at once." By December 2 when they started up Robidoux Pass the mules were shaking from cold. The saddlebags of corn were vanishing rapidly. Fremont, who had always insisted on a full day's march, had to call a halt early in the afternoon for the sake of the shivering animals.

On December 3, in the language of the Colorado trappers, "They took the mountain." They descended the Sangre de Cristo and came onto the floor of the San Luis Valley; it took the party four days to cross the snow-covered dunes and to reach the Rio Grande River, from where they moved to the mouth of Wagon Wheel Gap. Here in an evening conference at the base of the San Juan Mountains, facing straight up into the main assault of the Rockies, a serious dispute arose between Old Bill Williams and Fremont; and a decision was made which proved to be a death warrant not only for eleven men of the Fourth Expedition but subsequently for Old Bill himself.

Fremont was dissatisfied with Old Bill's choice, his instincts telling him that they were headed wrong, that they should turn at this point for Cochetopa Pass, which was less difficult of access. Old Bill swore that "he knew every inch of the country better than the Colonel knew his own garden." Alexis Godey, Fremont's second-in-command, writes:

"Williams was so strenuous in his efforts to carry his point, that I was completely in his favor, and told the Colonel that I myself was perfectly willing to trust Williams and follow him."

Fremont had no choice; what he did not know was that the route Williams proposed taking up to the Continental Divide, the Wagon Wheel Trail, had been his own discovery and was his favorite child.

From the first moment of their assault on the boulder-strewn, snow-packed Alder Canyon the Fourth Expedition's difficulties began: on this day the first mule died, others sinking down in the snow, their packs needing to be reset by men whose fingers were already frostbitten. At night the camping spot was so precipitous that it was impossible for the men to stay on their feet while unpacking the mules. They traveled through three to four feet of snow at the beginning, then snow up to the mules' bellies. Seven or eight miles of pushing upward was a tremendous distance to accomplish from sunrise to sunset, and after a fierce snowstorm struck, two hundred yards an hour was the maximum that could be achieved.

The third day the men and mules were obliged to stumble onward after dark to find any kind of tenable camp. Fremont and his mountain men began to suspect that Old Bill was lost. Already twenty days out of Hardscrabble, most of the corn was gone; the snow was twelve to fourteen feet in height through which the men had to beat a path by flailing ahead with their bodies and clubs. The weather was twenty below zero. The intense cold and high altitude made it painful to breathe. The men were bleeding at the nose.

The suffering of the mules was even greater. They cried all night in the bitter cold. Brandon describes them in *The Men and the Mountain:*

"By now they were skeletal creatures made of heavy flanks and yellow teeth, with mucus frozen at their eyes and nostrils and frozen scabs of sores hanging from their coats."

The men worked all day and much of the night to keep the mules alive. But they were dying slowly, their faces turned away from the storm, their heads sinking lower and lower until they fell.

For the men the passage of time was a continuous nightmare, unable to sleep for the thunder of the snow slides, the roaring gale and above it the pathetic crying of the mules. Yet no man faltered, their loyalty and dedication to Fremont holding firm in the midst of the death-dealing hell. On December 15 as they tried to force a ridge in the teeth of a howling gale and were thrust back, Old Bill lost consciousness while riding his mule.

On December 17 the party camped on the Continental Divide at 12,287 feet, the highest point they would come. They had one more valley to traverse, then up through the narrow Carnero Pass and down the west slope of the Rockies toward warmer climate and grass.

The next morning Fremont broke camp early. They were no sooner started than the worst storm of the journey struck, so fierce that no man could make a yard of progress against it. They were physically blown back into their camp on the crest of Wannamaker Creek.

Here for four days they dug into deep holes in the snow to fend off the howling storm. They spent their time butchering the mules who were dying. Here, on December 20, John Fremont at last admitted defeat, and gave the order for the party to turn back. Had they been able to leave the crest before this ultimate storm struck they could have made their way to Carnero Pass, and the final push would have taken them only a day or two past their twenty-five-day allotted span. Like the Donners, the Fourth Expedition was a matter of hours late.

John Fremont had to turn back, but he would attempt to save all of his equipment and scientific instruments for a future assault.

On December 22 he sent a relief party to make its way down out of the mountains to Taos to bring back supplies and fresh mounts. Three of the most experienced men volunteered, Old Bill, Creutzfeldt and Henry King, who had been with Fremont's former expeditions. Fremont asked Breckenridge to go along. He gave the party sixteen days to make Taos and to get back, while the rest of the expedition would be working its way down the mountains with the equipment, which they would have to carry on their backs.

A subtle form of disintegration now began to break up what had been a cohesive party. John Fremont had lost or abandoned his gift of leadership; he allowed the men to travel down the mountain in separate messes, spread over the trail by as much as seven to nine miles, with three hundred man-loads of equipment, each man carrying sixty to seventy pounds of weight. Fremont sometimes lost contact with the body of his men trailing behind him, the weakest and oldest bringing up the rear, all still living in the bitter cold with little to eat but frozen mule meat.

The first casualty came on January 9. Raphael Proue, trying to carry a pack across the open flats in what was described as perfectly unbearable cold, collapsed because his legs froze under him. Vincenthaler wrapped a blanket around him, but when he returned from having taken his pack to the river Proue had died. Micajah McGehee said:

"We passed and repassed his lifeless body, not daring to stop long enough in the intense cold to perform the useless ritual of burial."

Two days later, since the sixteen days which had been allotted for the relief party to return had passed, Fremont himself set out, not only to find his men, but to reach Taos and send back supplies. He took with him Godey, Preuss, Godey's nephew Theodore and Saunders Jackson, an ex-slave from the Benton household in Washington. He also took some food, a little sugar and tallow candles, leaving the same amount for the remaining twenty-five men.

Two days later he came upon his relief party. They had already eaten their footgear, their belts and knife scabbards, and could no longer travel on their frostbitten feet. Weak and almost unable to see from show blindness, the experienced Henry King had said, "I can go no further, I am sorry, but I am tired out, will sit here until I am rested. I will follow." When the others stumbled back later to see what had happened to him, he was dead, sitting where they had left him.

With the men left behind, despair set in rapidly. Fremont had appointed as their captain Vincenthaler, a man who was incapable of holding the group together for a last-ditch stand against their common enemy, death.

The men started down the Rio Grande River, their supplies consumed, and no game within sight. Teeth fell out of their mouths, their faces became black from the fires over which they crouched for warmth. Every small scratch became a running sore. They could make only two miles a day, even in the flat country. Henry J. Wise staggered a few feet and fell. Two of the Indian boys dug a shallow grave for him. A third of the Indian boys, Manuel, after having the rotted soles of his frozen feet fall off, laid down and died by the river. Next Rohrer died, insane, then Midshipman Elijah T. Andrews, a young and inexperienced traveler from St. Louis. On the twenty-sixth Benjamin Beadle, one of the veterans, died; then Carver from Illinois, then young George Hubbard from the Iowa border; then John Scott, all perishing of exhaustion and starvation. Every last shred of equipment was left behind on the mountains and the plain.

By the twenty-eighth of January eleven men, more than a third of the Fourth Expedition, were dead. The following day Alexis Godey came in with fresh mounts and Indian guides secured by Fremont in Taos. The remaining men were saved.

John Fremont borrowed money from old friends in Taos and offered to mount and take with him any members of the expedition who still wanted to go on to California, where he had planned to meet his wife Jessie and daughter Lily. While he had been struggling to conquer the icy Rockies they had been making their way to California, the first white women to cross the tropical jungle of Panama. Two years before, even as Fremont was starting on his return to Washington, riding in disgrace behind General Kearny, he had turned over to Thomas O. Larkin a sum of three thousand dollars with which to buy a fine piece of land called the Santa Cruz ranch, originally cultivated by the mission padres, with vines and orchards already bearing. Fremont had walked over this land with Larkin, and it was to this Santa Cruz ranch that the Fremonts were heading on their separate ways, to build a hearth and a home in California.

Several of the survivors of the expedition decided to accompany Fremont as he set out over the Old Spanish Trail.

Old Bill Williams and Dr. Kern went back into the mountains to retrieve some of the treasure lost there, and were never seen again.

The men had not matched the mountains.

The first of many human sacrifices had been made to the building of a transcontinental railroad to California.

Chapter XXXII

"How do we get to the gold?"

THE FORTY-NINER WAS AN OUT-OF-STATER who gave up his home, his job and his girl to "see the elephant," that is, experience the ultimate in adventure and hardship. Few knew anything about California. Few cared, for they were going to return home as soon as they had made their pile.

Forty thousand prospectors poured into California by the end of 1849. A handful returned home; the great body remained...with or without gold. About two fifths came by sea: the seventeen-thousand-mile journey around Cape Horn, or by sea to Chagres, across Panama on foot or muleback, and then up the Pacific coast, arriving in San Francisco after a seven months journey in good health though bored, in the same outfits that had so startled the people in the streets of New York: red flannel shirts, broad felt hats of a reddish-brown hue, loose coats reaching to their knees, high boots, revolvers and knives at their belts: veteran Californians even as they sailed into the bay.

Their first question as they waded across the shallow waters of the cove was: "How do we get to the gold?"

Their initial view of San Francisco was disenchanting. The lone brick building had encouraged few followers, tents and shacks still overwhelmed the solid structures, the streets were a funnel of dust in the heat and a swamp of mud in the rain. The city itself was in the throes of a political scandal, Alcalde Leavenworth having been suspended for misappropriation of funds, the sheriff raiding his office to seize the records. Prices were so high that a man could be shorn of his capital before he could get proper directions to the mines. One passenger caustically wrote home:

"Just arrived. San Francisco be damned!"

In 1848 seven hundred ships had sailed into San Francisco Bay, most of them being abandoned by crews that had signed on merely to get a free ride to the gold fields. The bay had become a stick-forest of masts as the ships rotted and sank slowly into the cove mud.

The greater portion of the Forty-Niners came overland, following the California trail blazed by the Bidwell-Bartleson, Chiles Walker, Kelsey, Bryant, Stevens, Grigsby-Ide, Clyman parties, twenty-five thousand men and over a hundred thousand animals working their way westward.

They were equally disenchanted.

By the time the parties reached Utah their supplies were low, their stock lean and tired, with the hardest part of the journey ahead. A portion of the Forty-Niners followed the Mormon Trail into Salt Lake, though many other trains avoided the Mormon city, depriving themselves of important help. Both sides were suspicious and frightened, the Mormons because the emigrant parties originated in Missouri where the Saints had suffered violence; the Forty-Niners because, though they had never laid eyes on a Mormon, they had been taught to believe that the Saints were the incarnation of evil.

Immediately the Mormons found the gentiles (Mormon word for everyone outside their religion) to be friendly, they offered the hospitality of Salt Lake, and there was trading of considerable advantage to both sides. The Saints bought the emigrants' extra solid rations and surplus tools, metals, mechanical equipment; the emigrants received fresh stock and repair services for their wagons. The Mormons asked high prices for their milk, butter and fresh vegetables, but also nursed the emigrant sick, sharing their homes with the trail-weary families and putting up quite a few for the winter, Brigham Young setting the example by offering the hospitality of his own home to incoming strangers.

It was not until the trains started across the desert that real suffering began, not only from thirst but from Asiatic cholera. The rains came into the valley of the Humboldt, which Fremont and Bryant had described as "a valley rich and beautifully clothed in blue grass and clover," and found that the stock of the increasing hordes had consumed all the blue grass and clover. Man and beast alike drank the sparse water. By autumn they were renaming the Humboldt the Humbug and the Hellboldt, one rhymster complaining of:

Scribbling asses
Describing nutritious grasses.

The ordeal of the desert, to be played to a climax a few months later by the Jayhawker and Manly parties on the scorching sands of Death Valley, was marked in the summer of 1849 by a trail of shallow graves, the bleaching skeletons of twelve hundred animals, of abandoned household goods, beds and bureaus, stoves and trunks, and finally of the wagons themselves, their canvas and staves bleaching like the white bones of played-out animals.

"The Humboldt was filled with what the Lord had left over when he made the world, and what the devil wouldn't take to fix up hell."

Water sold for $15 a glass, but only vinegar could cure a man's mouth of scurvy. One thousand wagons were abandoned within a distance of forty-two miles. The weaker folk went insane, one woman setting fire to their camp when her husband refused to turn around and go home. There were heroic marches, men who pushed ahead in the burning heat to find water and bring it back to dying men and animals. Every group except the very early and the very young left part of its family or some of its friends behind forever in the wastes.

When they did reach water and the eastern slope of the mountains, exhausted, rations gone, there was the formidable Sierra Nevada to be crossed, wagons to be hauled up the sides of cliffs, before they could enter the gold mines by following the rivers and canyons down from the seven-thousand-foot height to the mining camps. Little wonder that so few were willing to return home, with such an investment of suffering and fortitude. Their tears and blood had watered the mountains and the plains. California was to be theirs forever. Hulbert says in his *Forty-Niners*:

"The finding of gold is luck; you will not be held blamable if you are unlucky. But making the journey, overcoming obstacles, fighting your way through, that is a matter of grit, not luck. Do that, get there, and you are absolved, you have mastered the part of the game that depended on you."

Most of the Forty-Niners spent most of 1849 in travel; not until August and September did the overlanders begin to reach the mines. By the end of the year there were a hundred thousand people in California, of whom eighty thousand were gold-fever arrivals: eight thousand along the Old Spanish Trail into southern California and then north to the mines; nine thousand Mexicans, mostly from the border province of Sonora; forty-two thousand overland, almost entirely Americans, and thirty-nine thousand by sea, of whom twenty-three thousand were Americans.

The Forty-Niners who had come by ship were largely city men, described as "editors, ministers, traders, the briefless lawyer, starving student, the quack, the idler, the harlot, the gambler, the hen-pecked husband, the disgraced...." Then, as a sobering aside, Bancroft adds, "with many enterprising honest men and devoted women."

Those who set out from Missouri for the two-thousand-mile trek across plains, mountains and deserts were by contrast mostly farmers and mechanics who were accustomed to handling wagons and stock and living with the frontier.

Of the eighty thousand arrivals only forty thousand went into the mines, the others staying in the towns and settling the farms; exactly half the gold-fever arrivals making the long hard journey not to mine but to begin a new life in a new country which, they reasoned, must become rich and provide magnificent opportunities for all because of the millions in gold being pumped into the economy.

By fall the Forty-Eighter camp had been converted into the Forty-Niner town, five times as large as its antecedent, with the tents and lean-tos on the hillside giving way to cabins, stores, saloons and hotels on either side of a one-block street. The simple "pan" had given way to the larger and slightly more complex "cradle" or rocker. The Forty-Niner did not find gold paving on top of river streets; he had to use his pick and shovel in order to dig below the sand, raising a bumper crop of blisters. He found gold, over $20,000,000 worth of it in 1849, but with five times as many men digging, the ratio fell off to such an extent that one ounce a day was considered an average take, and many of the emigrants were forced to "mine for beans."

Spectacular finds were less common. The Forty-Eighters believed that the gold was inexhaustible; the Forty-Niners said the gold was there but that it would take hard work and luck to get it.

The atmosphere remained colorful. Vigorous young men in red shirts, pants stuffed in their boots, wearing beards and swathes of hair like sheep dogs constituted an all-male society: hard-working, -drinking, -swearing, -playing; the weaker ones coming down with everything from homesickness through scurvy and dysentery to rheumatism, typhoid, tuberculosis and smallpox. They were buried in their blankets. Doctors tiring of the unaccustomed physical labor of the mines had gone back to their practice, charging one ounce of gold per consultation and one dollar for a drop of medicine. There were still few women: at the dances the men matched to see which should be the ladies. On Sunday the men went down to the river to soap and pound their clothes.

"Have two shirts. Wear one until it is dirty. Hang on a limb exposed to wind, rain and sun. Put on second shirt. Wear until dirty. Then change to clean one."

The first laundresses to reach the mining towns made more money than their prospecting husbands.

Though some of the miners brought their violins or guitars, though they played cards to pass the time, though all holidays were riotously celebrated and elaborate practical jokes played, the Forty-Niners were lonely men isolated from the civilized world. A few had copies of Dickens, Homer or the Bible, but books were scarce and newspapers cost a dollar each. Their being away from home, family, friends and traditions accounted for the rapid success of the saloon and gambling hall, which garnered at least as much of the miner's gold as went into the rapidly developing general stores, grown from packs on mules and supplies sold from open wagons to wooden structures with proper counters where a man, for a price, could now buy anything.

"Preserved oysters, corn and peas at $6.00 a canister; onions and potatoes, whenever such articles made their appearance; Chinese sweetmeats and dried fruits; champagne, ale and brandy, sardines, lobster salad."

Life in the mining region in 1849 changed quickly from the Garden of Eden of 1848. Crime, of which the Forty-Eighter saw little, began to mount.

The age of chivalry had lasted only one short season. Though the English, Irish, Australians and Germans were quickly assimilated, and the Californios were liked, the Chileans and Sonorans respected for their mining skills, racial antagonism began to spring up among the thousands of strangers thrown together into a political vacuum. The Indians were run out of their mountains, the Chinese and Mexicans pushed out of the better claims, the French, called Keskydees from their omnipresent question, "*Qu'est-ce que se dit?*" ("What did you say?") remained clanish.

San Francisco became as colorful as any mining camp when the early rains poured down from the skies and the miners poured down from the freezing mountains. The clay streets became quagmires into which the city threw "loads of brush wood and limbs of trees; as a result mules stumbled in the streets and drowned in the liquid mud, and the possibility of being thrown because the horse's legs were entangled in the brush, was a constant dread." Sometimes horse and wagon were swallowed up, the owner barely escaping.

At the corner of Clay and Kearny a sign was posted:

This street is impassable;
Not even jackassable.

A whole cargo of stoves, worthless because so many had arrived at one time, was thrown into the sea of mud and served as excellent steppingstones...unless you happened to land on one of the lids and have it come off! -

From San Francisco too the brotherly atmosphere of 1848 had vanished. Among the thousands attracted by gold were men who had been problems back home in settled communities with working governments. This rough element ganged together under the name of The Hounds, and one night descended upon the defenseless colony of Chileans to beat them up, kill a few, and wreck their easily wreckable quarters. The city rose in its wrath to kick The Hounds out of town, reimbursing the Chileans for their losses.

It was a prologue to one of the most violent decades ever experienced by an American city.

CHAPTER XXXIII

New States for the Union

THE AMERICANS WHO CAME into the Far West had been born into self-government, absorbing its nutritious milk from their mothers' breasts and from the town pump as well. They knew how to set up their own government as surely as they knew how to practice their profession or craft. The twenty-five thousand Americans who came overland to California in 1849 voted their laws and traveled under their elected officials to such an extent that the migration has been called "a marching laboratory of political experiment." To these adepts at democracy the idea of living under a military government was unacceptable, even though amiable Colonel Mason issued few decrees and had even fewer troops with which to enforce them.

As early as December 11, 1848, a meeting had been held in San Jose expressing the need for a constitutional convention representing all of California. This meeting sparked others; in San Francisco, Sacramento, Monterey, Sonoma. On April 15, 1849, Brigadier General Bennett Riley, a sixty-one-year-old Marylander who had fought in the War of 1812, the Black Hawk and the Mexican wars, described by his contemporaries as "A grim old fellow and a fine, free swearer," with no experience whatever in governing, arrived to take over the civil governorship from Colonel Mason. When he learned that Congress, immersed in its near-bloody discussion of whether these new lands acquired from Mexico were to be admitted as slave or free, had adjourned without providing either statutes or government for California, he issued a call for a constitutional convention to take place in Monterey, asking that delegates be elected in August from every district.

California would set itself up as a state, even if Congress did not want it!

The California convention opened in Monterey on September 3, 1849, in a solid two-story, native yellow sandstone edifice which the Reverend Mr. Colton had built for a schoolhouse and assembly hall with funds raised from "town lots and gamblers' banks." Forty-eight delegates had been elected, from San Diego on the southern border to the most northerly mining camps on the Trinity River, toward the Oregon line.

Six of the delegates were Californios, representing the finest tradition of the Mexican period: Mariano Vallejo from Sonoma, Andres Pico from San Jose, Jose Carrillo from Los Angeles, Jose Covarrubias from Santa Barbara, Miguel de

Pedrorena from San Diego and Pablo de la Guerra of Monterey, whose beautiful and cultured wife made their home a gathering place for the delegates. Thomas O. Larkin also extended hospitality, as did Mrs. Jessie Benton Fremont in her charming Spanish house with enclosed patio.

Jessie, waiting in the Parker House in San Francisco, where she and John had planned to meet when they separated on the Missouri border, had been informed that her husband had perished in the snows of the Rockies. She was ill and despondent, yet certain within herself that this man was indestructible. He joined her more than a year after their parting.

To their stupefaction the Fremonts learned that Thomas O. Larkin had not bought the Santa Cruz ranch with the money John had given him, as he had agreed to do, but instead had bought for them a wild tract of land somewhere high in the Sierra Nevada called the Mariposa ranch. It was inaccessible, several hundred miles from the ocean or nearest settlement, several hundred miles from San Francisco, with no farming land, too wild and cold in winter even to graze cattle, and overrun with hostile Indians. Larkin explained that as Fremont's appointed agent he felt he had the right to use his own best judgment, that he did not believe Fremont would ever make a farmer, and that he had learned the soil on the Santa Cruz ranch was no good anyway. The Fremonts were further confounded to learn that Larkin had bought the Santa Cruz ranch himself: a rare, unexplained and equivocal act in the life of Thomas O. Larkin.

Having found themselves without farm or home, the Fremonts had made their way down to Monterey in the hot July sunshine, where they rented a beautiful Spanish home, and where Jessie prepared to hold open house for the delegates who would soon be assembling for the constitutional convention. It was the Fremonts' ambition that John should be the first senator from California. This would wipe out the disgrace of a court martial!

Of the thirty-seven American delegates at the convention, twenty-two came from free states, fifteen from slave; there were four, including John Sutter, who were born out of the country. It was a young man's convention, nine being under thirty, twenty-three under forty. Almost all of the early settlers were there: Thomas O. Larkin representing San Francisco; Joel Walker, Sonoma; Lansford W. Hastings, of the Hastings cut-off, represented Sacramento, rancheros from southern California such as Abel Stearns and Hugo Reid, the Scotsman who had married an Indian girl and planted excellent vineyards. Robert Semple of Benicia, who ran the ferry across the Carquinez Strait, was elected chairman; William Hartnell was named interpreter. There were fourteen lawyers, twelve farmers, seven merchants, a scattering of printers, engineers, bankers, doctors.

The outstanding personality of the convention was William Gwin of Tennessee, newly come to California with the express purpose of being elected one of California's first senators. He was described by a reporter as having "grandeur of exterior, magnificence of person, of herculean figure." He had something of greater importance, copies of the constitutions of New York and Iowa, having gone to the personal expense of having the newest state constitution, that of Iowa, printed in San Francisco so that each delegate might have a copy before him.

The most difficult problem of the convention was where California's eastern boundary should extend. The Gwin-Halleck proposal, which had considerable backing, suggested that California should consist of all the land acquired from Mexico by the Treaty of Guadalupe Hidalgo, that is, the entire Far West. When the actual maps were drawn, the group modestly contented itself with Nevada, the near half of Utah, which included all the Mormon settlements as well as that portion of Arizona embracing present-day Phoenix. The opposition claimed the area was too large to be manageable, and that it included thousands of Mormons who were not represented. The boundaries as sketched on one of Preuss's maps from Fremont's expedition led the delegates to set the eastern border in the Sierra Nevada, which traverses the greater part of the state.

The question of slavery in California never got started, the bill to forbid slavery passing unanimously. There were heated debates on whether dueling should be allowed (it was not); whether women should be allowed to control all property in their possession before marriage (they were). When it was proposed that all persons charged with criminal offenses be tried by a jury of their peers, one delegate shouted:

"What do we want with peers? This ain't no monarchy!"

The convention of near strangers went peaceably through the weeks, evolving a liberal constitution which provided for equitable taxation and a good educational system. Through Gwin's persuasive politicking, as well as the copies he had provided, the constitution of Iowa was largely followed. The Californians quickly waved aside the unworthy idea that they should ask for mere territorial status, informing the United States Congress that they were, and would be, a full-blown state.

On October 13, when the last of the delegates had signed the constitution, General Riley fired a thirty-one-gun salute because California expected to be the thirty-first state of the Union. John Sutter sprang to his feet and cried with tears streaming down his face:

"Gentlemen, this is the happiest day of my life...a great day for California!"

The delegates, aware of the millions in gold coming out of the mines, paid prodigally for all services. Each member received $16 a day plus $16 per mile traveled; $10,000 was appropriated for J. Ross Browne, clerk of the convention, to print the convention's report in English and Spanish; Governor Riley was to be paid at the rate of $10,000 a year as governor, Captain Halleck $6000 as secretary of state until the popular election.

The delegates then assessed themselves $25 each for a gala costume ball, held in the convention hall that evening to celebrate their creation of the new state, the delegates and Monterey society dancing most of the night unrepressed by the chill thought that Congress wanted no part of them.

The canvass for the approval of the constitution and for the election of the state officers was short; there had been so little time for electioneering that one miner exclaimed:

"When I left home I was determined to go it blind. I voted for the constitution, and I've never seen the constitution. I've voted for all the candidates, and I don't know a damned one of them."

All-seeing or blind, the constitution was approved, 12,061 to 811; Peter H. Burnett, one of Sutter's former assistants, was elected governor. General Riley proclaimed that military rule in California was ended.

When the legislature met on December 20, John C. Fremont was elected United States senator on the first ballot, and William M. Gwin on the third.

The character of John C. Fremont was beyond permanent defeat, as it was beyond permanent victory. Having ridden into the Sierra Nevada to inspect his seventy-square-mile totally useless ranch, he discovered gold; not merely "the color" or gold dust, not merely small nuggets that had been eroded by the weather and washed down by the rain and the streams to the valleys below. Here on the Mariposa John Fremont discovered a mother lode, a body of gold that had been cast up by the vast volcanic action which formed the mountains, veins of gold bedded in the rock of the mountainside.

Within a matter of a year after Fremont had acknowledged defeat on the summit of the Great Divide he became the single largest owner of gold in California, a millionaire, setting forth for Washington as the first elected senator from the fabulously rich and romantic California. He could not be seated until Congress admitted California as a state, but to the Fremonts as to all Californians this was an unimportant detail.

Thus, at the end of 1849, the government of California had been created, with representatives on their way to Washington to achieve statehood for the folks back home.

By the discovery of gold which cascaded a hundred thousand people into California in a little more than a year, there had been created a totally new phenomenon on the American political scene where territories had been settled slowly and painfully over a long period of years.

CHAPTER XXXIV

Statehood

B Y CONTRAST TO VIGOROUS SAN FRANCISCO and Salt Lake, Los Angeles of 1850 was standing still, a sleepy village of mud huts surrounded by extensive ranchos, without a public school, newspaper or library. With its hot, waterless, dusty near-desert climate, its main activity was fighting Indians who were raiding the ranchos, the Paiutes driving off as many as five hundred head of cattle. Two thirds of the population was illiterate; the one third that could read and write was busy sending petitions to Congress asking that southern California be separated from northern California and called the State of Central California, a separatist movement which was due to the feeling of the southern Californians that they had nothing in common with northern California. At the moment they were right.

Northern California was a lean hard-bitten mountain man, a Jedediah Smith or Joseph Walker fighting his way across the snow-clad Sierra Nevada with a hunter's gun slung on his back; male, rugged, disciplined, carrying the seed of a new civilization. Southern California was a lush, red-lipped, sensual female who came up from Acapulco in the cabin of a well-rigged Spanish ship, sunning herself in a patio surrounded by bougainvillea, her gown cut sufficiently low to intimate how abundantly the coming generations might be nourished.

San Francisans were beginning to take on the character of the perpendicular hills they had to climb, and the submerged grimness of the cold, foggy weather. They were a stony people, astonishingly like New Englanders: stubborn, proud, willful, self-contained, tenacious, fiercely independent, rooted in rocky tradition. The international flavor persisted, yet at the same time there was a curiously insular quality, almost like that of an island folk.

San Francisco's first theatrical season began on January 16, 1850, in Washington Hall, with the Eagle Theatre Company playing a farce and a drama. A few weeks later the National was opened, a proper theatre of brick, with a French company. The government was installed in its first City Hall, the former Graham House, a four-story wooden building on the corner of Kearny and Pacific, with four flights of continuous balconies overlooking the busy streets.

In May a fire broke out before dawn in a rickety gambling saloon; for several hours the wind-driven flames raced up and down the hills, burning three hundred houses, including the City Hall, two sides of Portsmouth Square and the three important business blocks. The loss was over $4,000,000, accounting for nearly half the gold dug out of California in 1849, making Brigham Young sound like a prophet when he told his Saints:

"The true use of gold is for paving streets, covering houses and making culinary dishes."

Within ten days half of the burned city was rebuilt, the first volunteer fire department organized and every home owner warned to keep six buckets of water on hand for future emergencies. It would not be quite enough; not even the five fire companies with pretentious names like the Empire Engine Company, the Protection or the Eureka could keep San Francisco from becoming the most frequently burned-down city in the world. On June 12, forty days later, a fire started in a broken chimney in the Merchants Hotel and the business district from Kearny Street to the waterfront burned down, another $3,000,000 vanishing in smoke; in September one hundred fifty houses burned, in October another $250,000 worth of property, including the city Hospital; in December there was a $1,000,000 loss of wood and corrugated iron wall buildings....

California was having an equally hard time becoming a state. On January 1, 1850, Senator John C. Fremont, his wife Jessie and their daughter Lily had boarded the S.S. *Oregon* in Monterey Harbor en route to Washington to have California admitted. They were rowed out to the ship by Indian boys in a torrential downpour of rain, but no greater than was the torrent of speeches which kept Fremont out of the Senate and California out of the Union through the spring and summer months until the South's unwillingness to admit another free state was compromised. Now on October 18, 1850, the S.S. *Oregon* sailed into San Francisco Harbor flying all its bunting and signaling that California had been admitted.

San Francisco promptly went wild. All business houses and courts were locked, guns began firing from the hills surrounding the city, bands and paraders stomped through the streets, the ships in the harbor broke out their flags, newspapers off the S.S. *Oregon* sold for $5.00 apiece. At night bonfires blazed from the peaks.

"Mounting his box behind six fiery mustangs lashed to the highest speed, the driver of Crandall's stage coach cried the glad tidings all the way to San Jose, 'California is admitted!', while a ringing cheer was returned by the people as the mail flew by."

Indeed, California had become the thirty-first state.

Some Source Notes on Quotations

Page

1 "commanded over by Colonel Vallejo," Zollinger, *Sutter*, 55-56.

1 "Well, my god," Ibid., 57.

1 "I noticed the hat must," Ibid.

3 "A large number of deer," Ibid., 66.

5 "I was insulted," Bancroft, *History of Cal.*, IV, 3.

6 "a Puritanic strength," McKittrick, *Vallejo*, 4.

10 "Kept guard over," Ibid., 20-21.

13 "Graham was the worst," Bancroft, IV, 7.

13 "noted for being a bummer," Ibid.

13 "about three o'clock," Ibid., 18.

21 "California is a country," Bancroft, IV, 212.

22 "We have also," Dakin, *Lives of William Hartnell*, 251.

24 "It is too late now," Zollinger, 101.

29 "The presidio of Monterey," De Mofras, *Travels*, 211-12.

26 "The state of Society," Wilkes *U.S. Exploring Exped.*, V, 198.

26 "compared the climate,"

Page

Ibid., 154.

26 "The country has," Ibid., 151-152.

26 "I was surprised," Ibid., 152.

27 "In his brilliant uniform," Zollinger, 112.

27 "The difficulty of coming," *St. Louis (Mo.) Daily Argus*, Oct. 31, 1840, 2.

29 "This is beyond all comparison," Ibid.

29 "a genius for invention," Hunt, *John Bidwell*, 22.

29 "Robidoux's description," Ibid., 35-36.

30 "purchase a suitable," Ibid., 36.

30 "Our committee fell to pieces," Ibid., 37.

31 "Compared to the trials," Ibid., 46.

31 "Started early," Ibid., 60.

31 "valleys between peaks," Ibid., 67.

32 "If I ever get back," Ibid., 66.

33 "they arrived here," Lyman, *John Marsh*, 249.

33 "The company has already," Hunt, 92.

34 "I was marched," Bidwell, *Echoes of the Past*, 72, 73.

37 "Streams were out," Hunt, 96.

37 "As long as he had anything,"

Page

Zollinger, 113.

37 "He was one of those," Ibid., 114.

39 "Carson and Truth," Nevins, *Fremont,* 101.

39 "There is no man," Ibid.

41 "The unsettled state," Bancroft, IV, 301.

42 "This change in the aspect," Ibid., 310.

43 "I may forfeit," Ibid., 306-7.

45 "Myself again having been honored," Hastings, *Emigrant's Guide.*

50 "scenery very wild," Fremont, *Memoirs,* 189-90.

50 "To explore unknown regions," Cleland, *This Reckless Breed,* 283.

53 "We continued down the valley," Fremont, 309.

53 "This mighty range," Ibid., 152.

54 "Rock upon rock," Ibid., 155.

54 "Far below us," Ibid., 333.

54 "There is the little mountain," Ibid.

61 "He was born," Stewart, *Opening of the Cal. Trail,* 40.

63 "The poor footsore oxen," Ibid., 67.

66 "a tilted cap," Dana, *Sutter,* 162.

67 "In case I should be killed,"

Page

Zollinger, 143.

71 "It will no doubt," Larkin Papers, IV, 4.

72 "The route I wished," Fremont, 432.

72 "It had never before," Carson, *Own Story.*

72 "Nearly upon the line," *Fremont,* 432-33.

72 "a sandy, barren plain," Nevins, 213.

73 "The Mexican troops," Larkin Papers, III, 266.

73 "The future destiny," Ibid., IV, 44-45.

74 "Why is an American," Ibid., 185.

75 "In the afternoon," Fremont, 459.

75 "moved up the mountain," Ibid.

75 "If we are attacked," Nevins, 228.

75 "a band of robbers," Ibid., 229.

77 "I held a confidential," Nevins, *Polk,* 22.

77 "In addition to your Consular," Larkin Papers, IV, 4-6.

78 "Has not enjoyed," Ibid., 302.

78 "I have seen his name," Zollinger, 193.

78 "Being absolved from any duty," Nevins, *Fremont,* 247.

Page

79 "I saw the way," Fremont, 490.

80 "Almost the whole party," Bancroft, V, 111-12.

80 "Gentlemen, what is it," McKittrick, 261.

83 "I am also informed," Fremont, 519.

85 "Captain Fremont," Nevins, *Fremont*, 277.

86 "I have determined," Hittell, *Hist. of Cal.*, VII, 463.

89 "wearing a buckskin," Colton, *Three Years in Cal.*, 32.

89 "Our bay is full," Ibid., 85.

90 "The custom had been," Ibid., 41.

90 "as chaste," Ibid., 43.

90 "Law which fails," Ibid., 66.

90 "If there is," Ibid., 48.

97 "A more ragged," Nevins, *Fremont*, 300.

97 "I feel myself," Bancroft, V, 426.

100 "Put spurs to your mules," DeVoto, *Year of Decision*, 302.

100 "The Californians were," Ibid., 307.

101 "It is barely possible," Ibid., 180.

102 "There is a nigher route," Ibid.

103 "Two days and two nights," Stewart, *Ordeal by*

Page

Hunger, 42.

105 "The trap which closed," Ibid., 87.

106 "they stripped the flesh," Ibid., 133.

108 "in sight," Ibid., 248.

113 "an old school gentleman," Zollinger, 218.

114 "It is hard to conceive," Ibid., 227.

115 "The river here flowed," Parsons, *Marshall*, 53-54.

116 "Having strolled," Ibid., 56-57.

116 "Boys, by God," Zollinger, 236.

117 "There! Didn't I tell you," Ibid., 234.

119 "I have made a discovery," Bancroft, VI, 43.

120 "We have found gold," Zollinger, 243.

121 "The instrument of discovery," Caughey, *Gold Is the Cornerstone*, 16.

122 "Gold!" Bancroft, VI, 56.

122 "A general of the United States Army," Colton, 248.

122 "A frenzy seized my soul," Caughey, 22-23.

123 "everyone has gold... fever," Underhill, *From Cowhides to Golden Fleece*, 168.

123 "My sons," Bancroft, VI, 65.

126 "The miners needed," Shinn,

Page

Mining Camps, 112.

127 "no man shall grumble," Ibid., 107.

128 "Cursing the country," Bancroft, VI, 96.

128 "Confer on them," Ibid., V, 611.

129 "People are running," Ibid., VI, 114-15.

129 "The accounts of the abundance," Caughey, 42.

131 "Well authenticated accounts," Soule, *Annals of San Fran.*, 210.

132 "We pay at the rate," Colton, 279.

132 "We cannot imagine," Underhill, 168.

134 "Indians, Negroes, Kanakas," Zollinger, 263-64.

143 "Just arrived," Caughey, 91.

144 "a valley rich," Ibid., 115.

144 "Scribbling asses," Ibid., 116.

144 "The Humboldt," Hulbert, *Forty-Niners*, 214.

145 "editors, ministers," Caughey, 45.

146 "mine for beans," Ibid., 174.

146 "Have two shirts," Ibid., 183.

147 "This street is impassable," Asbury, *Barbary Coast*, 13.

149 "a marching laboratory," Caughey, 107.

149 "a grim old fellow," Bancroft, VI, 275.

Page

151 "Gentlemen, this is the happiest," Ellison, *Self-Governing Dominion*, 44.

154 "The true use of gold," Werner, 256.

154 "Mounting his box," Bancroft, *Hist. of Cal.*, VI, 348.

Index

For a free catalog of California regional titles, or to order an additional copy
of this book, please call 1-800-497-4909